The Complete Guidebook to Yosemite National Park

"On the whole, Yosemite is incomparably the most wonderful feature on our continent."
—A. D. Richardson

✳ **by Steven P. Medley**

1991 EDITION

YOSEMITE
ASSOCIATION

Contents

DEBRA KNODEL

Design and maps by
    Jon Goodchild/Triad.
Illustrations by Bob Johnson.
Produced by US National Parks
    Publishing Co.

Printed in Korea.

Cataloging in Publication Data

Medley, Steven P., 1949—
The Complete Guidebook to Yosemite National Park/by Steven P. Medley.
    112p.   cm.
    Includes bibliographic references and index.
ISBN 0-939666-55-3
    1. Yosemite National Park (Calif.)—Guide-books.
F868.Y6M48   1990
917.94 ′ 47053—dc20

Yosemite Association
P.O. Box 545
Yosemite National Park,
California 95389

Help Make This a Better Guidebook!

We are eager to hear your reactions to this book, and welcome your suggestions for additions or changes. Please send your comments, criticisms and ideas to the Yosemite Association.

Further Reading

You may purchase any of the books mentioned in this guidebook from the Yosemite Bookstore which operates sales facilities at Visitor Centers throughout the park. The bookstore also carries many more titles, maps, guidebooks and videos which have Yosemite as their subject. Call or write to place your order or to request a publications catalog.

Yosemite Bookstore
P.O. Box 230
El Portal, CA 95318
(209) 379-2648

Thanks to everyone who helped in the production of this book including Pat Wight, Penny Otwell, Claire Haley, Holly Warner, Gail Dreifus, Anne Steed, Mary Vocelka, Jim Snyder, Linda Eade, Len McKenzie, Dean Shenk, Marla LaCass, John Poimiroo, Laurel Munson, Mallory Smith, Craig Bates, N. King Huber, Jan Van Wagtendonk, Peter Browning, Jim Alinder, Bill Neill, Tony Secunda, Hal Belmont, Gideon Sorokin, Mono Lake Committee, Yosemite Park & Curry Co.

Cover photographs by William Neill.

YOSEMITE
ASSOCIATION

For Jane and the boys

"From the discovery of Yosemite to the present day, the wonders of this region of sublimity have been a source of inspiration to visitors, but none have been able to describe it to the satisfaction of those who followed after them."
—Lafayette Bunnell

"You've got a good point, Lafayette, but here goes anyway . . ."—S P M

STEPHEN LYMAN

Major Features of Yosemite Valley

Ribbon Fall
Echo Peaks
Eagle Peak
Mount Watkins
Basket Dome
El Capitan
Three Brothers
North Dome
Tenaya Canyon
Washington Column
Clouds Rest
Quarter Domes
Mirror Lake
Merced R
Su
M

Major Features of Yosemite National Park

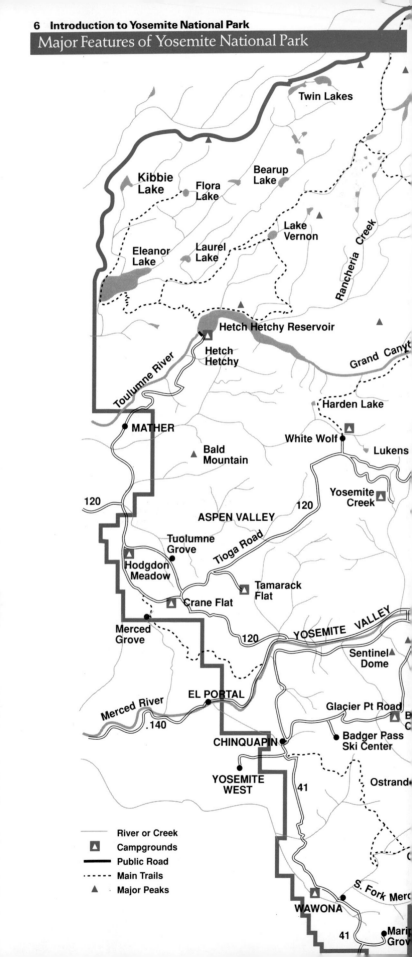

Twin Lakes

Kibbie Lake

Flora Lake

Bearup Lake

Lake Vernon

Eleanor Lake

Laurel Lake

Rancheria Creek

Hetch Hetchy Reservoir

Hetch Hetchy

Toulumne River

Grand Canyon

Harden Lake

MATHER

White Wolf

Lukens

Bald Mountain

Yosemite Creek

120

ASPEN VALLEY

120

Tuolumne Grove

Tioga Road

Hodgdon Meadow

Tamarack Flat

Crane Flat

YOSEMITE VALLEY

Merced Grove

120

Sentinel Dome

EL PORTAL

Glacier Pt Road

Merced River

.140

CHINQUAPIN

Badger Pass Ski Center

YOSEMITE WEST

41

Ostrande

S. Fork Merc

WAWONA

41

Marip Grov

Legend

- River or Creek
- ▲ Campgrounds
- Public Road
- - - - Main Trails
- ▲ Major Peaks

Soldier Lake

Spiller Lake

Smedberg Lake

McCabe Lakes

Mt Conness

120

mne

Glen Aulin High Sierra Camp

Dog Lake

Mt Dana

Tioga Pass

t Lakes

ay Lake h Sierra Camp

120

Tuolumne Meadows High Sierra Camp

Elizabeth Lake

Cathedral Peak

Evelyn Lake

Lyell Canyon

Tenaya Lake

Sunrise High Sierra Camp

Vogelsang High Sierra Camp

Merced Lake

Bernice Lake

Mt Lyell

High Sierra Camp

Mt Clark

Ottoway Lakes

Edna Lake

Chain Lakes

nson ke

Buck Camp

Yosemite by the Numbers

Yosemite National Park

Established: October 1, 1890

Size: 748,542 acres, or 1,169 square miles. 94% of the park is designated wilderness.

Address: P.O. Box 577, Yosemite National Park, CA 95389

Campsites: 1,982 parkwide

Overnight Accommodations: 1,738 units

Paved Roads: 360 miles

Developed Trails: 800 miles

Wildlife Species (approximate):
Amphibians & Reptiles – 40
Birds – 242
Fish – 11
Mammals – 77

Flora Species:
Flowering Plants – 1,400
Trees – 37

Highest Peak: Mt. Lyell, 13,114 ft.

Geographic Center of the Park: Mt. Hoffmann

Highest Paved Pass in the Sierra: Tioga Pass, 9,941 ft.

Major Park Lakes:
With Fish – 127
Without Fish – 191
Total Lakes – 318

Rivers and Streams: 880 miles

Park Speed Limit: 45 MPH

Yosemite's Ten Highest Peaks

1. Mt. Lyell – 13,114 ft.
2. Mt. Dana – 13,053 ft.
3. Rodgers Peak – 12,978 ft.
4. Mt. Maclure – 12,960 ft.
5. Mt. Gibbs – 12,764 ft.
6. Mt. Conness – 12,590 ft.
7. Mt. Florence – 12,561 ft.
8. Simmons Peak – 12,503 ft.
9. Excelsior Mountain – 12,446 ft.
10. Electra Peak – 12,442 ft.

Entrance Fees

Private, Noncommercial Vehicles: $5.00
Bus Passengers, Bicyclists, and Persons on Foot or Horseback: $2.00
Annual Yosemite Pass: $15.00
Golden Eagle Pass *(good at all National Parks for the calendar year):* $25.00
Golden Age Pass *(for U.S. citizens age 62 years and older):* free

TTY Phones

These numbers allow hearing impaired persons with their own TTYs to call the park directly.
National Park Service Information
(TTY) 372-4726
Room Reservatons
(TTY) 255-8545

Important Yosemite Phone Numbers

Unless otherwise noted, all phone numbers in the following list and throughout this book are for the (209) Area Code.

Weather and Road Information
372-4605
General Park Information
372-0264
Campground Information
372-0302
Recorded Camping Information
372-4845
National Park Service
372-0200
Yosemite Bookstore
379-2648
Yosemite Valley Visitor Center
372-0299
Big Oak Flat Visitor Center
379-2445
Tuolumne Meadows Visitor Center
372-0263
Wawona Ranger Station
375-6592
Yosemite Room Reservations
252-4848
High Sierra Camp Reservations
252-3013
Ticketron Camping Reservations
1-800-452-1111 ($4 handling charge)
Medical Clinic
372-4637
Dental Clinic
372-4200
Lost and Found
372-4720

Park Visitation

1855 – 42
1899 – 4,500
1922 – 100,506
1940 – 506,781
1954 – 1,008,031
1967 – 2,201,484
1989 – 3,429,619

If You Have Only One Day in Yosemite . . .

Three things only are well done in haste: flying from the plague, escaping quarrels, and catching flies. — H.G. Bohn

If by some horrible twist of your itinerary you find yourself with but a single day in Yosemite National Park, you will be sorely cheated. The park is so large and so studded with fascinating features that usually 3 or 4 days are required to really "do the place justice." But take heart for there are some remarkable highlights which can be enjoyed in a day, many of them centered in Yosemite Valley.

Yosemite Valley

While Yosemite Valley's seven square miles comprise but a tiny fraction of the park's total area, they are jam-packed with spectacular scenic beauty. First of all, get out of your car (follow signs to day-use parking at Curry Village) and board a free Yosemite Valley Shuttle Bus. Buses access practically every point of interest in the eastern end of Yosemite Valley, and are the only means (besides bicycle or on foot) to enter the areas there that are closed to automobile traffic. Listed below are several activities that can be enjoyed in a day from stops along the Shuttle Bus route. See page 24 for more Free Shuttle Bus information.

✳ **Valley Visitor Center:** Here is a logical starting point for your visit. See page 24. Park information, orientation, exhibits and books are all available here. If time allows, take in the Yosemite Museum Gallery, the Indian Cultural Exhibit, and walk through the Indian Village behind the center. (15 minutes to 1 hour)

✳ **Lower Yosemite Fall:** Walk from the bus stop to the base of Lower Yosemite Fall — about a quarter of a mile. See page 30. Be prepared to get wet in spring when runoff is at its peak; in any season you'll be impressed by the imposing height of one of the world's most famous falls. (30 minutes to 1 hour)

✳ **Happy Isles:** This is the trailhead for hikes to Vernal and Nevada Falls, Half Dome and other high country destinations (except in winter). See page 31. Walk to the Vernal Fall bridge (seven tenths of a mile) for a breathtaking view of this beautiful cataract or continue on to the top of the fall (if you've got the energy). This route is known as the Mist Trail for reasons that will be obvious. During the summer, the Happy Isles Family Nature Center offers exhibits and books. (1 to 3 hours)

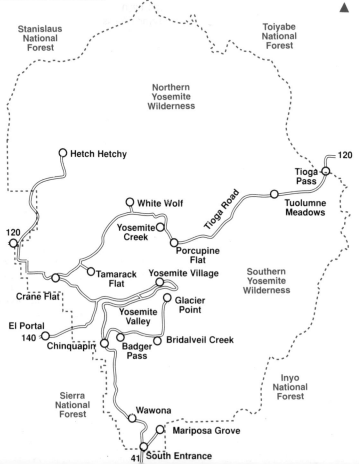

North

Stanislaus National Forest

Toiyabe National Forest

Northern Yosemite Wilderness

Hetch Hetchy

120

Tioga Pass

White Wolf

Tuolumne Meadows

Tioga Road

Yosemite Creek

120

Porcupine Flat

Tamarack Flat

Yosemite Village

Southern Yosemite Wilderness

Crane Flat

Glacier Point

El Portal

Yosemite Valley

140

Chinquapin

Badger Pass

Bridalveil Creek

Inyo National Forest

Sierra National Forest

Wawona

Mariposa Grove

41 South Entrance

❋ **Mirror Lake:** From the shuttle bus stop (not accessible in winter), Mirror Lake is a half mile walk up a slight grade. See page 30. While the lake no longer offers the mirror-like surface for which it was named (it's filling up with silt), one of the best views of Half Dome is had from its banks. The hike around the lake is easy and rewarding. (1 to 2 hours)

When you've seen and done all you want by shuttle bus, you will need your car to finish up in Yosemite Valley. For a thoroughly entertaining treatment of the remaining sights, an audio tape program entitled *Yosemite Audio Guides: Yosemite Valley Tour* is available for sale at the Visitor Center and heartily recommended. The tour consists of 10 stops and, besides descriptions of the scenery, features discussions of the geology, native American culture, history and park management. The tape is exceptionally well-produced. Using it, you will require from 2 to 4 hours for your tour depending on how much exploring you do at each stop.

If you don't use the tape, there are at least two more Yosemite Valley points to visit:

❋ **Bridalveil Fall:** Follow road signs to Highway 41 (to Fresno). Immediately after turning on to Route 41, turn left into the Bridalveil Fall parking lot. The short trail leads to the base of the fall where a sheet of water floats downward 620 feet to the Valley floor. See page 75 for more information. (15 to 45 minutes)

❋ **Tunnel View:** Turn left back onto Highway 41 and drive approximately three miles to Tunnel View turnout, which is just below the entrance to the Wawona Tunnel. Before you is the classic panoramic view of Yosemite Valley that greeted the first visitors here. (10 to 30 minutes)

Glacier Point

A 32 mile drive from Yosemite Valley, Glacier Point is unquestionably a "must see" for visitors with limited time. Within 200 yards of the parking lot is the top of the sheer southern wall of Yosemite Valley. Not only does the valley lie 3200 feet below you, but the entire park is revealed with astounding vistas in every direction. All of Yosemite's major peaks are identified, and exhibits explain the geologic processes

that created this amazing landscape. There is probably no better view of Yosemite Valley and the surrounding high country that can be reached by automobile. The road to Glacier Point is closed in winter. See page 44 for more information. (1 hour for the drive from Yosemite Valley, and 30 minutes to 1 hour at Glacier Point)

Mariposa Grove of Big Trees

If you have already seen Yosemite Valley and Glacier Point and you've still got time (hard to believe!) the Mariposa Grove of Big Trees is located near the park's south entrance on Highway 41. See page 46. This magnificent stand of sequoias is Yosemite's largest and includes trees thousands of years old. A tram system transports visitors into the grove for a fee (from May to October), or you may enter on foot (the hike into the upper grove area is fairly rigorous, however). A small museum is open during the summer (the tram stops there), and famous trees like the Grizzly Giant and the fallen Tunnel Tree should not be missed. (2 to 3 hours)

Tuolumne Meadows and the Tioga Road

Open in summer only, the Tioga Road bisects the park and leads through Tuolumne Meadows, a beautiful subalpine meadow surrounded by soaring granite crags and polished domes. See page 63. If your trip takes you out of the park to the east, the Tioga Road is lined with scenery and exhibits describing it. See page 58. Be sure to stop at Olmsted Point which provides a remarkable view of Tenaya Canyon and the back side of Half Dome, and of Tenaya Lake, the deep blue, icy cold waters of which form one of Yosemite's largest lakes. (Allow 2 to 2 and a half hours for the trip from Yosemite Valley to Tioga Pass)

Just Passing Through?

If it happens that you are simply driving through Yosemite (a regrettable situation), be sure to pick up a copy of the *Yosemite Road Guide* which will provide an added dimension to your drive. It is keyed to markers along park roads and describes the sights, gives historical information, and is full of data about Yosemite's plants and animals.

Lodging in Yosemite

Most overnight accommodations in Yosemite are operated by the Yosemite Park and Curry Co., a contractor of the National Park Service and the park's chief concessioner. There is a single reservation system for all Curry Co. lodging units. Whenever a Yosemite hotel or motel is not part of the Curry reservation system, that fact will be noted in this guidebook.

Reservations may be made by phone or mail. The main YP&CCo. reservation number is (209) 252-4848. Because thousands of calls are made to this number each day, you may not get through when you phone. Be persistent, let the phone ring, and try, try again.

If you're unsuccessful with the phone, try sending your reservation request in writing. Fill out the form provided below and mail it to: Yosemite Reservations, 5410 E. Home, Fresno, CA 93727. Be sure to indicate acceptable alternatives as competition for popular dates is heavy.

Nine Tips for Getting a Yosemite Reservation

1. Public reservations for Yosemite lodging open exactly 366 days in advance. Call (209) 252-4848 immediately upon the opening of the Yosemite Reservations office (8 am, Pacific Time) exactly 366 days before your intended arrival.

2. Choose to visit in Yosemite's off-season, particularly the months of November, January, February and March. You're sure to be accommodated if you elect to come during the week. There's a special winter reservation number: (209) 454-2000.

3. If you want to stay over a weekend, plan your arrival for a Monday, Tuesday, Wednesday or Thursday. You can reserve up to seven nights in a row in any given stay. Often, lodging facilities are fully reserved for weekends earlier than 366 days in advance by people arriving earlier in the week.

4. Be flexible and have several arrival dates in mind. If your first option is not available, one of the others may be.

5. If you're willing to stay in a tent cabin at Curry Village, request it. Tent cabins are in the least demand and can usually be reserved up to two weeks before arrival. And when you arrive, you can always try to upgrade to a room with bath (but there are no guarantees here).

6. Call Yosemite Reservations on Saturday or Sunday. The office receives the fewest number of calls on weekends.

7. Don't call at lunch. Everybody tries to call then.

8. Call 30 days, 15 days or 7 days in advance of your arrival. These are common times when rooms held by previous reservations are cancelled. You may get lucky.

9. If you arrive in Yosemite without a reservation, stop by the front desk of any lodging facility between 10 am and 4 pm and place your name on the waiting list. Persons with reservations that are held without a deposit must confirm or arrive by 4 pm. If they don't, their reservations are cancelled automatically. If you are present at 4 pm, you may pick up a cancelled reservation or you may not.

Reservations for Lodging

Reservation Request Form (please print).

Name:

Address: Phone:

City: State: Zip:

Number in Party: Children: Ages:

Preferred accommodation:

Date of Arrival: Date of Departure:

No. of Nights:

2nd Choice, if preference is unavailable:

Mail to: Yosemite Reservations,
5410 E. Home, Fresno, CA 93727.

Camping in Yosemite National Park

Yosemite National Park offers visitors over 2,000 campsites in its multiple campgrounds. If you're planning to camp, be sure to secure an authorized spot because camping is allowed only in designated campsites. Even if you've got a "self-contained" recreational vehicle, you are not permitted to pull off to the side of the road for the night. Neither should you erect your tent or throw down your sleeping bag wherever you stop; the rangers will send you packing. The impact on the park resources of such haphazard camping is too great.

Fortunately, there's a way to insure that you'll have a Yosemite camping spot when you arrive. The majority of park campsites can be reserved through a campground reservation system administered by Ticketron. Throughout this guidebook and in the chart which accompanies this text, campgrounds with sites which can be reserved through Ticketron are indicated.

How to Reserve Your Campsite

You may reserve Yosemite campsites through Ticketron in three different ways: in person at any Ticketron outlet (check your phone book), by mail, or over the telephone. To reserve by mail, fill out a copy of the form provided here and mail it to: Ticketron, Box 62429, Virginia Beach, VA 23462.

For telephone reservations, you should call 1-800-452-1111. Ticketron adds a $4 handling charge for each transaction placed by phone. Thirty operators begin taking calls at 10 a.m. Pacific Time each day.

Please note the following important condition: you may make Ticketron campsite reservations no more than eight weeks in advance for regular campsites and no more than twelve weeks in advance for group campsites.

For additional information about park campgrounds, refer to the following pages:
Yosemite Valley, *page 32.*
South of Yosemite Valley, *page 49.*
North of Yosemite Valley, *page 66.*

Camping in US Forest Service Areas Adjacent to Yosemite

The US Forest Service operates a variety of campgrounds near Yosemite. Many of them are operated on a first-come, first-served basis; some sites may be reserved through the MISTIX reservation system. For additional information call the appropriate USFS district office.

☀ Inyo National Forest
Eastern Sierra, Highways 120 & 395
Mono Lake Ranger District
  (619) 647-6525

☀ Sierra National Forest
Western Sierra, Highways 140 & 41
Bass Lake Ranger District
  (209) 683-4665
Mariposa Ranger District
  (209) 966-3638

☀ Stanislaus National Forest
Western Sierra, Highway 120
Groveland Ranger District
  (209) 962-7825

Campsites in Yosemite National Park

Campground/general location	# of sites or spaces	daily fee; per site = /s per person = /p	RV space	tent space	tap water	stream water (boil)	flush toilets	pit toilets	tables	fire pits or grills	pets allowed	dump station	parking	showers nearby	laundry nearby	groceries	swimming	fishing	horseback riding	camping season (approximate)	Notes
North Pines Yosemite Valley	86	$12/s	●	●	●		●		●	●			●	●	●	●	●	●	●	May–Oct	Ticketron
Upper Pines Yosemite Valley	240	$12/s	●	●	●		●		●	●	●	●	●	●	●	●	●	●	●	Mar–Nov	Ticketron
Lower Pines Yosemite Valley	173	$12/s	●	●	●		●		●	●			●	●	●	●	●	●	●	all year	Ticketron
Upper River Yosemite Valley	124	$12/s	●	●	●		●		●	●			●	●	●	●	●	●	●	Apr–Oct	Ticketron
Lower River Yosemite Valley	139	$12/s	●	●	●		●		●	●			●	●	●	●	●	●	●	Apr–Nov	Ticketron
Sunnyside Walk-In Yosemite Valley	38	$2/p		●	●		●		●	●			●	●	●	●	●	●	●	all year	First come basis.
Backpackers Walk-In Yosemite Valley	25	$2/p		●	●		●		●	●			●	●	●	●	●	●	●	May–Oct	First come basis. **2.** No vehicles.
Wawona Highway 41 in Wawona	100	$7/s	●	●	●		●		●	●	●		●			●	●	●	●	all year	First come basis.
Bridalveil Creek Glacier Point Road	110	$7/s	●	●	●		●		●	●	●		●				●	●		Jun–Sept	First come basis.
Hodgdon Meadow Highway 120 near Big Oak Flat	105	$10/s	●	●	●		●		●	●	●		●							all year	Ticketron May–Oct, $7 per site Nov–April
Hetch Hetchy Backpacker Hetch Hetchy Reservoir	19	$2/p $30/s		●	●	●	●		●	●			●				●	●		April–Nov	First come basis. Two group sites, two stock use sites. Backcountry users only. No RV.
Crane Flat Highway 120 near Tioga Road turnoff	166	$10/s	●	●	●		●		●	●	●		●			●				May–Oct	Ticketron
Tamarack Flat Tioga Road	53	$4/s		●		●		●	●	●	●		●							Jun–Oct	First come basis. No RV.
White Wolf Tioga Road	88	$7/s	●	●	●		●		●	●			●	●			●		●	Jun–Oct	First come basis.
Yosemite Creek Tioga Road	75	$4/s		●		●		●	●	●	●		●							Jun–Oct	First come basis. No RV.
Porcupine Flat Tioga Road	55	$4/s	●	●		●		●	●	●	●		●							Jun–Oct	First come basis. Limited RV.
Tenaya Lake Walk-In Tioga Road	50	$7/s		●	●			●	●	●	●		●				●	●		Jun–Oct	First come basis.
Tuolumne Meadows Tioga Road	330	$10/s	●	●	●		●		●	●	●	●	●	●		●	●	●	●	Jun–Oct	Ticketron, half camp sites same day reservations. 25 walk-in sites with no vehicles, $2 per person.

Ticketron: reservations required. **2:** Two night-max. No RV: Access Road not suitable for large trailers or large RVs.

Campsite Reservation Request

Please include middle initial in your name:

Name:

Address:

Zip:

Telephone:

No. of Persons: Pet(s): ☐ Yes ☐ No

Important: Reservations may be made eight weeks in advance for individual campsites. Reservations may also be made by telephone. Complete this form and then call: 1-800-452-1111. Ticketron adds a $4 handling charge for each transaction placed by phone.

Be sure you complete all sections and enclose full payment. Incomplete or incorrect forms will be returned.

Type of camping equipment:

Check ✓		♿
1	One tent or no equipment	17
2	Two tents	18
3	Large tent (over 9' × 12')	19
4	Tent trailer	20
5	Van or bus with side tent	21
6	Pickup/camper thru 18'	22
7	Pickup/camper thru 21'	23
8	Motorhome thru 24'	24
9	Motorhome thru 27'	25
10	Motorhome over 27'	26
11	Trailer thru 15'	27
12	Trailer thru 18'	28
13	Trailer thru 21'	29
14	Trailer thru 24'	30
15	Trailer thru 27'	31
16	Trailer over 27'	32

Golden Access or Golden Age Passport Serial No. if applicable:

Not Golden Eagle Passport or Park Pass.

Charges: The daily campsite charge is required for each period and/or campsite.

No. of nights _____ @ _____ * _____ = _____

No. of nights _____ @ _____ * _____ = _____

No. of nights _____ @ _____ * _____ = _____

*50% reduction for Golden Access or Golden Age passport

Total: _____

☐ Check ☐ Money Order ☐ MasterCard ☐ VISA

Card No.: _____   Exp: _____

Cardholder: _____   Telephone: _____

Signature: _____

Make payable to Ticketron and mail to: Ticketron, Box 62429, Virginia Beach, VA 23462.

	First Choice:		Second Choice:		Third Choice:		Office Use:
Name of Park:	Arrival Dates:	Nights:	Arrival Dates:	Nights:	Arrival Dates:	Nights:	Nights:
Campground:							

So How's the Weather?

You don't need a weatherman to know which way the wind blows.— John Muir

Yosemite's climate is as mild as its cliffs are steep. The months of April through October feature warm daytime temperatures and cool nights. Even winter is relatively benign with average maximum temperatures in Yosemite Valley (4,000 feet) in the high 40's and 50's. Of course weather is significantly affected by elevation, and with a topography ranging from 2,000 to 13,000 feet in height, Yosemite can experience amazing climatic variations on any given day!

Precipitation averages 35 to 40 inches of moisture annually, with the greatest bulk of that falling between December and March. Snowfall in Yosemite Valley averages 29 inches but rarely accumulates to a depth of over two feet. At 7,000 foot Badger Pass, there is adequate snow pack to support a downhill ski area, and cross-country skiing is popular throughout the higher regions of the park.

As temperatures warm in the spring, increasing runoff swells rivers and creeks producing a grand display of surging waterfalls. There is negligible precipitation during the summer months, and many of the park's waterfalls literally dry up. Only occasionally do dramatic vernal thunderstorms bring renewed life, however briefly, to these seasonal water shows.

Yosemite Valley in Winter

The first falls of snow in the Sierra generally occur in November, but they do not come to stay; they are but fleeting messengers, and having announced the approach of winter, are soon put to flight by the lingering god of the tropics, who still tries to maintain supremacy over his rival of the Arctic Zone. But it is his final effort to keep back the legions of the north. By the end of December snow hides from sight all but the forms of the mountains, covering them with a vast winding sheet. Only the mighty trees toss from their wind-shaken branches the white deposit, which ofttimes with its unyielding weight snaps their great boughs.

Owing to the retreat of the sun southward, and the immense height of the walls of the Yosemite, there is a considerable difference between the climate on the north and south side of the valley during the winter. While on the south wall the sun never shines during this season, and a chilling shadow is constantly cast over that portion of the valley, the rays of the winter sun fall upon the surface of the northern elevation almost at right angles with its plane. As a consequence, the weather on that side is mellow and mild, and in sheltered nooks among the warm rocks flowers are observed to bloom every month in the year.

From *Foley's Yosemite Souvenir & Guide* for 1913 by D.J. Foley.

Temperature and Rainfall

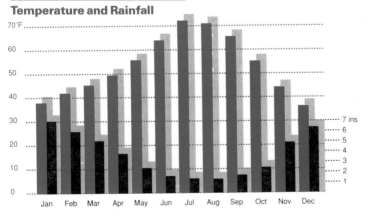

Yosemite Valley Weather

	January	April	July	October
Hours of Sunshine	3:57	7:38	9:34	6:45
Chances of a Sunny day	39%	70%	97%	81%
Afternoon Temperatures	48°	66°	90°	75°
Relative Humidity	86%	69%	50%	64%
Chances of a Dry Day	74%	80%	97%	94%
Total Precipitation	6.8"	3.3"	0.4"	1.5"
Snowfall	25.4"	4.5"	—	0.2"

Comment: High-country conditions are significantly cooler and much snowier during the winter months.

Backpacking in Yosemite

Because there are 800 miles of trail in Yosemite ranging through some of the most stunning scenery in the world, backpacking is a popular activity in the park. It allows its practitioners a true wilderness experience, and is really the only way large areas of Yosemite can be accessed.

But successful, minimum impact backpacking requires good physical health, knowledge of backpacking techniques, proper equipment, and a respect for the natural world. Uninformed backcountry users can cause great harm to the wilderness and not even know it. What follows are basic tips for backpackers, backcountry regulations, and sources for further information.

Get a Wilderness Permit

Wilderness permits are required for all overnight stays in Yosemite's backcountry. These free permits may be obtained at any of the following locations in the park: Yosemite Valley Visitor Center (see page 24), Tuolumne Meadows Permit Kiosk (just off the Tioga Road on the road to Tuolumne Lodge), Wawona Ranger Station (see page 40), Big Oak Flat Visitor Center (see page 56), and Hetch Hetchy Entrance Station for those using Hetch Hetchy trails (see page 55).

Reservations are accepted by mail only between February 1 and May 31. Send a brief itinerary to the Backcountry Office, Box 577, Yosemite National Park, CA 95389. Up to fifty percent of the capacity of each trailhead is available for reservations. The remainder of the daily quota is filled on a first-come, first-served basis, and permits may be picked up no more than 24 hours prior to trailhead departure. Reservations are especially recommended for hikes leaving from Tuolumne Meadows or with destinations of Little Yosemite Valley or Half Dome.

For trips originating outside the park, contact the US Forest Service. Quotas exist for many Forest Service entries into Yosemite, and permits should be obtained from the USFS station closest to your entry point.

Q: How fast can a backpacker carrying a pack that's one-fifth his or her body weight expect to travel?
A: About two horizontal miles per hour. Add one hour for each 1,000 feet of elevation gain.

Backcountry Regulations

✳ **Group Size:** Maximum group size in the Yosemite wilderness is 25 people on trails and 8 people maximum for any off-trail travel.

✳ **Campsite Location:** Please use an existing campsite at least 100 feet from lakeshores and streams to minimize pollution and vegetative impact. Camp four trail miles from Tuolumne Meadows, Yosemite Valley, Glacier Point or Wawona, and at least one trail mile from any road.

✳ **Human Waste:** Bury human waste in a small hole at least 100 feet from any lake, stream or camp area. Toilet paper should be burned or packed out.

✳ **Garbage:** Pack out all garbage (no exceptions). Do not bury garbage, scatter organic waste or leave foil in campfire sites.

✳ **Fires:** Wood fires are not permitted above 9,600 feet due to firewood scarcity. Use only existing fire rings and dead and down wood in areas below 9,600 feet.

✳ **Pets:** Dogs and other pets are not allowed in the Yosemite backcountry. They import diseases harmful to wildlife, annoy fellow hikers, scare stock and harass wildlife.

✳ **Soap:** Putting soap, including biodegradable soap, or any form of pollutant into lakes or streams is prohibited. Discharge washing and rinsing water at least 100 feet from water sources.

✳ **Firearms:** Firearms are not permitted in the backcountry.

✳ **Structures:** The construction of rock walls, fireplaces, bough beds, tables or lean-tos is prohibited.

Route Planning Information

Space considerations prevent a listing of even some of the thousands of trips that can be made into Yosemite's backcountry. But never fear, there are many resources available to help with your route planning task. There are a number of fine trail guides which can be consulted, and every year new and better maps are produced for the park. You can obtain maps or any of the trail guides listed on page 17 from the Yosemite Association at one of its Visitor Center bookstores or through the mail by writing PO Box 230, El Portal, CA 95318 or calling (209) 379-2648.

Backcountry Tips

✳ **Treat the Water:** Unfortunately, microscopic organisms known as *Giardia Lamblia* (see page 86) are present in backcountry lakes, rivers and streams. They can cause illness (sometimes quite severe), so you should not drink from these sources without first treating the water. Your options are to boil it for three minutes, to use a chemical disinfectant like iodide or chlorine (less effective than boiling), or to use a Giardia rated filter available from outdoor equipment stores.

✳ **Acclimatize:** Many backcountry trips begin at elevations much higher than you may be accustomed to, and then go even higher. It's a good idea to arrive a day early to let your body adapt to the thinner air. Don't overexert and drink plenty of fluids to avoid altitude sickness.

✳ **Outsmart the Bears:** Bears and humans regularly interact in Yosemite's backcountry, and in practically every instance, the bears are intent on sampling human food. To make sure that your interaction is a positive one, learn to properly hang your food. You'll need stuff sacks and at least 50 feet of rope or cord to manage the somewhat complicated but very effective counterbalancing method. You'll receive a pamphlet outlining the procedure when you get your wilderness permit.

✳ **Abandon Your Car:** To cut down on your driving and on overflowing parking lots at trailheads, consider using the Hiker's Bus service which operates daily from Yosemite Valley between July 1 and Labor Day. Buses travel the Tioga Road to Lee Vining, and to Glacier Point and the Mariposa Grove, with return trips each day. You can arrange to be dropped off or picked up at trailheads along most park roads. Call 372-1240 for more information.

✳ **Hang your food** and anything with an odor as instructed by the NPS. Hang pots and pans from food bags as an alarm. Sleep 20 to 30 feet from where your hang items so you can hear the bear and scare it away as quickly as possible. Keep some rocks available to throw.

✳ **If a bear approaches** your camp, act immediately to scare it away. Yell and make as much noise as possible. Throw rocks at the bear. Make more noise and chase the bear. Multiple people chasing a bear increases effectiveness.

✳ **Always maintain a safe distance** Do not advance on a bear which appears to feel threatened or cornered by you. Do not attempt to retrieve food or gear from a bear until the item is abandoned.

✳ **Food taken by bears** is your responsibility. Please clean up and report all bear damage to a ranger. Improper food storage can result in the killing of conditioned bears, personal injury, and property loss. Please do your part to keep Yosemite wild.

Further Reading

✳ *Yosemite National Park: A Natural History Guide to Yosemite and Its Trails* by Jeffrey P. Schaffer. Berkeley: Wilderness Press, 1989.

✳ *Yosemite Trails* by Lew and Ginny Clark. San Luis Obispo, CA: Western Trails Publications, 1976.

✳ *High Sierra Hiking Guides for Hetch Hetchy, Tuolumne Meadows and Yosemite* by various authors. Berkeley: Wilderness Press, various dates.

✳ *Guide to the John Muir Trail* by Thomas Winnett. Berkeley: Wilderness Press, 1984.

Bear-Proof Your Campsite!

Yosemite's black bears are clever and very persistent. If you fail to set up your camp and store your food properly, your whole trip can be ruined. Always follow the steps as follows:

Yosemite Climbing

Because of its vertical granite landscape, Yosemite is mecca for rock climbers from all over the United States and the world. Yosemite Valley has been the location of so many climbing developments and innovations that it has become the yardstick against which all other climbing areas are measured. In every season of the year, climbers can be seen clinging to rock faces or hanging by their hands and feet from upward-leading cracks.

Passionate rock climbers populate a world foreign to most "normal" people, and have developed a subculture with customs, clothing, language and tools of its own. In Yosemite, that world revolves around Camp Four (known on signs and maps as Sunnyside Campground). Hard by the Yosemite Lodge gas station, Camp Four is the climbers' permanent temporary home. Many of the hard core climbers move to Tuolumne Meadows during the summer.

Not that long ago, climbers utilized many artificial techniques to accomplish their climbs. These included drilling holes in the rock and inserting permanent metal bolts, chiseling holds in the rocks, and hammering in steel "pitons" that damaged the rock and might not be removable. Such steps made certain routes climbable that might not otherwise be.

Today, a less destructive and harmful climbing ethic has developed. Bolts are placed much less often, chiseling is frowned upon, and high-tech devices like "chocks," "friends" and "cams" (which are inserted into cracks and removed easily) provide protection for modern climbers. It's known as clean climbing, and it's a matter of high priority for climbers who wish to protect and preserve a natural, non-artificial climbing environment.

One interesting aspect of the climbing subculture is its system of naming and rating climbing routes. The first climber to successfully undertake a new path up a section of rock (a "first ascent") is entitled to name that route. That climber, and those who come after, also attempt to rate the difficulty of climbing that route. The Yosemite Decimal System is used for this purpose and is an elaborate scale with ratings from 5.0 to 5.13 with grades from "a" to "d" at each level signifying different degrees of difficulty to the climbing community.

Climbs range from short routes of 50 feet or less (a pitch) to multi-day ascents of Yosemite's biggest walls (like El Capitan) which are made up of many pitches. Many practitioners of the sport are now engaged in what's known as "free soloing." Not recommended for other than the finest, most skilled climbers, free soloing is the climbing of rocks without the assistance and protection of a climbing partner. Generally, no ropes are used, no climbing devices are attached to the rock, and no one will be there to catch you if you fall. Most of Yosemite's largest rock landmarks have been "free soloed" in less than a day.

The technology of climbing has advanced considerably over the past two decades. Special ropes made from synthetic fibers are used which stretch to absorb the weight of a falling climber. Their strength under pressure has also increased. Shoes covered with sticky rubber which adheres to practically any surface are now commonly used. And the devices mentioned above like cams and friends made from high-strength alloys have expanded climbing opportunities as well.

But good equipment or not, climbers must still have the skill and strength to climb the rocks. The mastery that has been achieved by many "rock jocks" is astounding, and routes that many once considered unclimbable are now accomplished almost daily. New routes are being explored and climbed, and other climbing firsts, like paraplegic Mark Wellman's 1989 ascent of El Capitan, continue to occur.

Rock climbing is not recommended for the casual park visitor. If you would like to learn more about the sport, consider taking a climbing lesson from the Yosemite Mountaineering School either in Yosemite Valley (call 372-1244) or in Tuolumne Meadows (call 372-1335). Without proper equipment and without proper technique, you could severely injure yourself or die. Do not, repeat, do not attempt rock climbing on your own without some formal instruction.

Ten Best-Named Climbing Routes on an Animal Theme

1. Doggie Submission (5.10b)
2. Fish Fingers (5.11b)
3. Gilligan's Chicken (5.7)
4. Ilsa She Wolf of the S.S. (5.10c)
5. Landshark (5.12a)
6. Pigs in Space (5.12)
7. Poodle Bites (5.10c)
8. Pterodactyl Terrace (5.9)
9. Realm of the Lizard King (5.11c)
10. Spank Your Monkey (5.10b)

A Ranger is a Ranger is a . . .

Oh, the ranger's life is full of joys,
And they're all good, jolly, care-free
*   boys,*
And in wealth they are sure to roll and
*   reek,*
For a ranger can live on one meal a
*   week.*
  — Anonymous

Yosemite National Park is administered by the US National Park Service (NPS), an agency of the Department of the Interior established in 1916. As a bureaucracy based loosely on a military model, the NPS is characterized by a complex ordering of job ranks and by its distinctive field uniforms. The green pants, grey shirt and universally recognized "Smokey the Bear" hat have become the trademark of the park ranger.

The key descriptor here is "park" as park rangers differ from forest rangers. Forest rangers work for the US Forest Service, a branch of the US Department of Agriculture, in National Forests throughout the country. While the job duties of park and forest rangers are often similar in their respective situations, park rangers work in parks and monuments, and forest rangers work in _____ (you fill in the blank!).

Now that you're able to recognize that the person in the flat-brimmed hat before you is a park ranger working in a national park, things start to get a bit more complicated. The National Park Service is divided into any number of departments ranging from visitor protection to interpretation to maintenance to resources management to administration. To confuse things, employees of the different divisions all wear roughly the same uniform.

The traditional park ranger is employed by the Division of Visitor Protection with duties that include law enforcement, traffic regulation, search and rescue, emergency medical treatment, and many others. In order to work as a traditional (or "real") park ranger, one must take special training and earn a law enforcement commission.

Park interpreters (interpretive rangers) are responsible for the educational program at Yosemite and give walks, talks and programs. They, too, are "real" rangers, but they generally have not been commissioned and do not perform law enforcement functions. Their uniforms are identical to those of protection rangers (except they don't carry guns and handcuffs).

Identical, too, are the outfits of the various park administrators like the Superintendent (the park's chief administrative officer), Assistant Superintendent, Chief Ranger, and other division chiefs. An easy way to distinguish these management types is by their lack of muscle tone and general overweight condition. Desk jobs can be brutal.

Things get a little more confusing with certain maintenance, fire and resource management workers. They've got the green pants, ditto the grey shirt, but instead of the funny hat, they wear dark green baseball caps with the NPS arrowhead insignia. These employees are not technically rangers, but their roles at Yosemite are equally significant and their contributions considerable.

Most people don't realize that the National Park Service has "exclusive jurisdiction" over Yosemite National Park. That means that state, county and local agencies do not operate and provide almost no traditional services here. In Yosemite there are no highway patrolmen, no sheriff's officers, no state or municipal firemen, no state courts, and no incorporated local government. These services fall to the National Park Service which very ably manages the park.

Please remember while you're in the park that if you need help of any kind (from emergency assistance to information), all uniformed NPS personnel are there to be of service.

Yosemite in the Winter

Many have the impression that when the first day of winter arrives in Yosemite, the whole place closes up tight until spring. They are mistaken, however; the park and its residents do not hibernate. Yosemite only "closes" when deep snowfall makes it impossible to plow access roads (which is almost never).

There are notable park changes in winter, but most of them add to the unique qualities of this special season. Much of Yosemite wears a covering of snow, and once-thundering waterfalls quiet themselves in frozen dormancy. The Tioga and Glacier Point Roads close, and visitor activities center on such winter sports as skiing and skating.

Weekdays in winter are perfect for experiencing Yosemite in a less-crowded, more serene environment. Yosemite Valley daytime temperatures can be surprisingly mild, and winter walks are some of the best. The biggest reward of all, however, is the sheer beauty and grandeur of a trans-figured Yosemite and its surrounding high country.

The major routes to the park remain open throughout the year. The roadway least affected by the weather is Highway 140 which leads from Merced via Mariposa and through the Arch Rock Entrance to the park. Highways 120 (from the west) and 41 are also excellent routes, but they are more often subject to closure from heavy snowfall, and many times require the use of tire chains. The roads in Yosemite Valley are plowed throughout the winter.

Winter driving in Yosemite requires special precautions. Because roads are regularly covered with ice and snow, driving speeds should be reduced. Always carry tire chains in your vehicle and obey the chain requirement signs. Watch out for snowplows, and never stop in the roadway (find a pullout where traffic can safely pass).

Skiing

Both cross-country types and downhillers will discover ski opportunities in Yosemite. California's oldest operating ski area, Badger Pass, is located at 7,300 feet about 45 minutes from Yosemite Valley on the Glacier Point Road. It's primarily a "family" oriented operation with ten runs and lots of ski lifts. Badger is an ideal place to learn to ski, and a ski school is available to enable that process. Free shuttle buses to Badger Pass are provided during the winter from lodging facilities in Yosemite Valley (and from other points on busy weekends). Call (209) 372-1330 for information about Badger Pass and the shuttle.

Several miles of both groomed and ungroomed trails for cross-country skiers also originate at Badger Pass. Tracks are laid out the Glacier Point Road all the way to Glacier Point, and skating lanes are also provided. Well-signed trails lead into the backcountry and out to the south rim of Yosemite Valley. The cross-country ski school at Badger offers classes, individualized instruction, and guided tours. Phone (209) 372-1244 for details.

A variety of services is available at the Badger Pass Ski Lodge. Ski rentals (both downhill and cross-country), ski repair, child care, and food and beverage service are all offered. There's also

a locker room and restrooms. The National Park Service staffs a ranger station primarily as a first aid facility in the A-frame building at Badger. The phone number is (209) 372–0409.

Another popular cross-country ski area is Crane Flat located at the intersection of the Big Oak Flat and Tioga Roads 17 miles from Yosemite Valley on Highway 120. There are no services provided here, but the meadows and forests are full of trails for skiers and snowshoers both.

Snowshoeing

You can showshoe on your own wherever there's adequate snow (at Badger Pass, Crane Flat or the Mariposa Big Trees, for example), or enjoy a ranger-led showshoe walk where the snowshoes are provided. Walks are presented several days a week from in front of the A-frame at Badger Pass, and reservations are required. Check the *Yosemite Guide* or call (209) 372-0299.

Ice Skating

A large outdoor ice rink is operated daily in Yosemite Valley at Curry Village (weather permitting) from November through March. It features a smooth, refrigerated skating surface, rental skates, a warming hut with lockers, a fire pit and snack stand. For hours and rates call (209) 372-1441.

Snow Play

Provisions have been made for individuals and families with a passion for sledding, tobogganing, inner-tubing, and snow play generally. The designated area for these activities in Yosemite is at the Crane Flat Campground on Highway 120 near its intersection with the Tioga Road. Another good snow play area is found just south of the park on Highway 41 at Goat Meadow in the Sierra National Forest. Supervise children well, and be careful. Many snow play related injuries occur every year.

Camping

There are four campgrounds in Yosemite that are open for use during winter. In Yosemite Valley, both Lower Pines Campground (see page 33) and Sunnyside Walk-In Campground (see page 33) have been winterized, and Upper Pines may be opened as needed. The Wawona Campground (see page 49) is the winter camping area south of the Valley, and in the north end of the park, it's Hodgdon Meadow Campground (see page 66). Reservations are required for Lower Pines Campground (follow the procedure detailed on page 12), while all others are first-come, first-served.

Backcountry Ski Huts

For the intrepid wilderness skier, two different huts are operated in Yosemite's backcountry. Nine miles from Badger Pass to the south of the Glacier Point Road is the Ostrander Lake Ski Hut. Set on the banks of a deeply frozen lake and below scenic Horse Ridge, the hut can accommodate up to 25 skiers overnight. There are beds with mattresses, cooking facilities, bathrooms, a wood stove and water. Run by the Yosemite Association, the Ostrander Ski Hut is so popular that reservations are required. Call (209) 379-2317 for details, or write Ostrander, PO Box 230, El Portal, CA 95318.

The second hut is located at Glacier Point and is reached by skiing the 10 miles out from Badger Pass to the end of the Glacier Point Road. It is operated by the YP&CCo. which also requires reservations. Beds and meals are provided, and a guide will accompany you and do the cooking. To learn more about the Glacier Point Hut call (209) 372-1244.

Junior Snow Rangers

The National Park Service offers a winter version of the Junior Ranger program (see page 28). By attending various ranger programs and completing a series of requirements, children can earn Junior Snow Ranger certificates and patches. Check the *Yosemite Guide* or stop by a visitor center for details.

The Bracebridge Dinner

Perhaps Yosemite's most long-standing winter tradition is the Bracebridge Dinner. A multi-course Christmas feast is presented at the Ahwahnee Hotel in the context of a colorful pageant based loosely on Washington Irving's *Sketch Book* account of a typical Yorkshire Christmas dinner in the manor of Squire Bracebridge. The music, costumes, food and drama combine for an unforgettable experience. Tickets for the event are quite expensive, but there's an enormous waiting list for them. Application must be made to the YP&CCo. by January 15th each year. Call (209) 372-1489 for an application, or write to 5410 E. Home Avenue, Fresno, CA 93727.

Old-Fashioned Christmas in Wawona

Each year the interpretive rangers in Wawona sponsor a number of holiday activities for visitors. They include caroling, storytelling, building tours, tree-trimming, stage rides, and other programs at the Pioneer Yosemite History Center. For specific times and dates, check the *Yosemite Guide* or call (209) 375-6391.

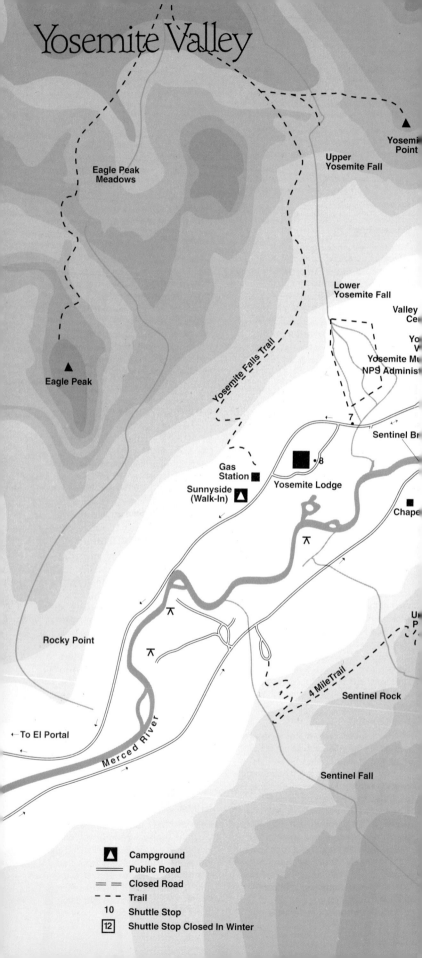

Yosemite Valley

Eagle Peak
Meadows

Upper
Yosemite Fall

Yosemi
Point

Lower
Yosemite Fall

Valley
Ce

Yo
V
Yosemite Mu
NPS Administ

Eagle Peak

Yosemite Falls Trail

7

Sentinel Br

Gas
Station

8

Yosemite Lodge

Sunnyside
(Walk-In)

Chape

Rocky Point

U
P

4 Mile Trail

Sentinel Rock

← To El Portal

Merced River

Sentinel Fall

Campground

Public Road

Closed Road

Trail

10   Shuttle Stop

12   Shuttle Stop Closed In Winter

Yosemite Valley is truly the heart of the park. With its granite monoliths, towering waterfalls, and pastoral meadows, the Valley is unique in the world for its remarkable scenery. Its seven square miles make up only a small fraction of the park's entire area, but 75 to 80 percent of the visitors to Yosemite spend their time in the Valley.

Not surprisingly, this popularity results in crowded conditions on popular weekends and during the summer. Campgrounds fill, concessioner accommodations become completely reserved, and day users clog Valley roads and parking lots. Efforts have been made to reduce the congestion caused by such heavy use, and some improvements have resulted.

Among them are a one-way road system, the closure of roads to automobile traffic in the east end of the Valley, development of an extensive network of bicycle paths, and the implementation of a shuttle bus system which links most developed areas in eastern Yosemite Valley.

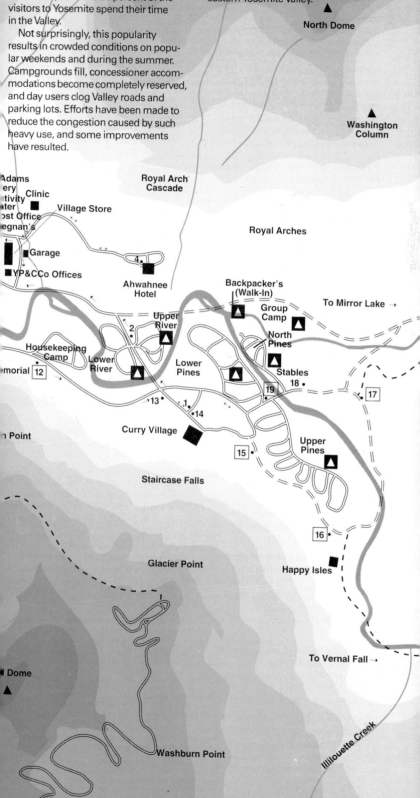

North Dome

Washington Column

Adams ery tivity ter Clinic
ost Office egnan's
Village Store
Garage
YP&CCo Offices

Royal Arch Cascade

Royal Arches

Ahwahnee Hotel

4.

Backpacker's (Walk-In)

Group Camp

To Mirror Lake →

Upper River

North Pines

2

Housekeeping Camp

Lower River

Lower Pines

Stables

18

19

17

memorial 12

13

1
14

Curry Village

15

Upper Pines

n Point

Staircase Falls

16

Glacier Point

Happy Isles

Dome

To Vernal Fall →

Washburn Point

Illilouette Creek

Can You Find the Visitor Center?

Lots of visitors come to believe, after hours of searching, that the Yosemite Valley Visitor Center has been purposely hidden from them. In many national parks, the first place you are directed by prominent signs is the parking lot in front of the Visitor Center. Not so in Yosemite Valley. Here you must either possess a Doctorate in nuclear physics or have experience as a Green Beret to make your way to "Information Central."

It really is worth taking the time to find the Visitor Center because it's the ideal place to start your visit. There you will find an orientation slide program, interesting exhibits, information services provided by knowledgeable rangers, and a complete bookstore. Near the Visitor Center are an Indian Cultural Exhibit and Indian Garden, plus a Museum Gallery with new exhibits hung regularly.

There's a good reason why the Visitor Center is so hard to find. Until 1971, a large paved parking lot at the Center's front door was accessible to automobiles. But given the tremendous congestion that was occurring in the Yosemite Village area and the desire on the part of the National Park Service to begin to eliminate private vehicles from the Valley, a decision was made to close the parking area and develop a pedestrian mall. The Visitor Center, for very good reasons, suddenly became unreachable by car.

But don't despair, you can still get to the Visitor Center by shuttle bus, bicycle or walking. Here's how to manage it from selected Valley locations.

❊ **From Day-Use Parking (Curry Village):** Park your car here and board one of the free Yosemite shuttle buses headed to Yosemite Village (bus stop #1). Get off the bus at Yosemite Village (bus stop #3). Take the flat, easy walk up the mall (to the west) about 200 yards to the Visitor Center.

❊ **From the Pines Campgrounds:** Jump on a shuttle bus at the stop nearest to you (bus stops #15, #18 and #19 are all close), and disembark at Yosemite Village (bus stop #3). The Visitor Center is 200 yards to the west up the mall.

❊ **From the Rivers Campgrounds:** Catch the free shuttle bus at bus stop #2 and get off it at Yosemite Village (bus stop #3). The Visitor Center is a 200 yard walk to the west up the mall.

❊ **From Housekeeping Camp:** The shuttle bus stops right in front of the entrance to the camp (bus stop #12). Take it and get off at Yosemite Village (bus stop #3). Walk 200 yards to the west up the pedestrian mall to the Visitor Center.

❊ **From the Ahwahnee Hotel:** It's about a 15 minute walk along the Ahwahnee Meadow and past the Church Bowl to the Visitor Center. Or take the free shuttle bus from in front of the hotel (bus stop #4) and get off at the Visitor Center (bus stop #6).

❊ **From Yosemite Lodge:** Catch the free shuttle bus in front of the Lodge registration area (bus stop #8). It will drop you off a few yards from the Visitor Center's front door (bus stop #9). The walk from Yosemite Lodge to the Visitor Center is less than a mile, and it's flat and easy and affords lots of good views along the way.

❊ **From the Parking Area behind the Village Store:** Walk around or through the Village Store to the pedestrian mall on the other side of it. Turn to your right and walk approximately 200 yards up the mall to the Visitor Center.

❊ **From the Parking Area behind Degnan's:** Walk around Degnan's to its front entrance on the pedestrian mall. Walk west up the mall the 100 yards to the Visitor Center.

These directions should make it clear that the key to finding the Visitor Center is locating the Yosemite Village mall. The Center is located at the mall's west end. If you're on your bicycle, bike trails are well marked and signs will direct you to Yosemite Village and the Visitor Center.

Free Shuttle Bus Rides

The easiest way to get around in Yosemite Valley (and to get out of your car and avoid traffic) is to ride, free of charge, the Yosemite Valley shuttle bus system. With stops at just about all locations in the eastern end of the Valley, the buses run every ten minutes or so (somewhat less frequently in the winter) and access areas such as Happy Isles and Mirror Lake which are closed to private automobiles. All the shuttle bus stops are indicated on page 22. In winter, shuttle service is discontinued to stops 16, 17, and 18.

Q: Where was the original Visitor Center (park headquarters) located in Yosemite Valley?

A: In old Yosemite Village, across from the present-day Yosemite Chapel just west of Sentinel Bridge.

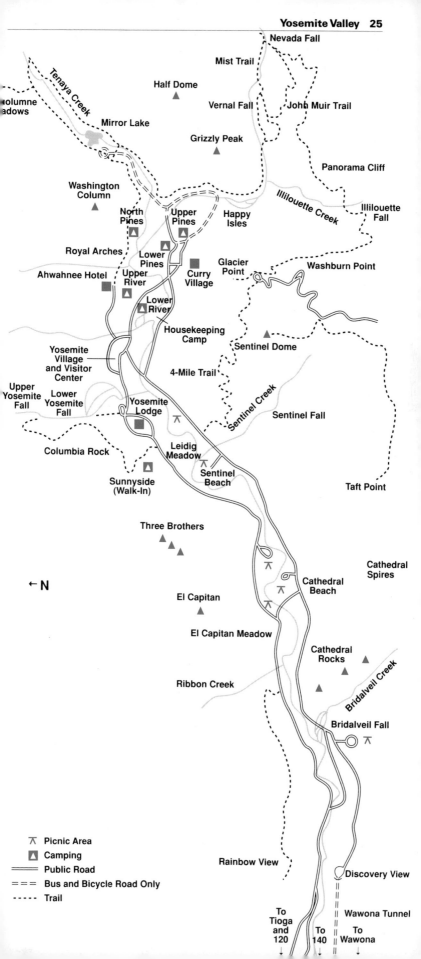

Best Bets in Yosemite Valley

✻ **The view from Glacier Point.** From the railing at Glacier Point, you are lord (or lady) of all the Yosemite you survey. The view is unforgettable. See page 37.

✻ **John Muir in person.** Noted actor Lee Stetson regularly portrays John Muir in dramatic presentations at the Visitor Center. It's Yosemite Theater at its best. See page 29.

✻ **A browse through The Ansel Adams Gallery.** This classy shop has been a leading Yosemite establishment since 1902. If you're a photographer, consider this your headquarters in the park. See page 22.

✻ **The hike to Vernal Fall.** An amazingly popular trip, but for good reason. The walk is essential Yosemite: rock, light and water at their most spectacular. See page 30.

✻ **A seat at Bracebridge Dinner.** This lavish Christmas pageant is held annually at the Ahwahnee Hotel and features much delicious food, seasonal music and elaborate costumes and decorations. See page 21.

✻ **Breakfast at The Ahwahnee.** It's a delight any time of the year to start your day with a casual yet luxurious breakfast in The Ahwahnee's grand dining room. See page 34.

✻ **The panorama from Tunnel View.** This classic Yosemite viewpoint never ceases to take one's breath. From this spot the Valley's geologic origin couldn't be more evident. See page 37.

✻ **A visit to the Visitor Center Bookstore.** Nowhere else in the universe has such a complete collection of books and other materials related to Yosemite and the Sierra Nevada been assembled in one place. See page 24.

✻ **Lower Yosemite Fall in springtime.** When the snows of the Yosemite high country begin to thaw, the results are a revitalized Yosemite Falls. Liquid thunder! See page 30.

Activities in the Valley

Once you have spent some time at the Visitor Center (page 24), there are unlimited possibilities for visitor enjoyment. Most of them involve seeing and learning about the amazing sights that Yosemite Valley has to offer.

Enjoy a Ranger Program

Throughout the year, park interpretive rangers present a wide variety of programs, walks, demonstrations, campfires, slideshows, films and talks. There is no charge for these activities, which occasionally do require reservations. Consult the *Yosemite Guide* for the daily schedule for these programs.

Visit Yosemite Valley's Eastern End

The free shuttle bus route takes visitors to the area of Yosemite Valley that is no longer accessible by private automobile. Such locations as Happy Isles which is the trailhead for the hikes to Vernal and Nevada Falls and Half Dome, and Mirror Lake can only be reached by the shuttle bus or on bicycle and foot. Excellent views of such landmarks as Glacier Point, Half Dome, Tenaya Canyon and Washington Column are afforded from stops along the way. This section of the shuttle bus route is closed in winter.

Make a Circle Tour of the Entire Valley

To reach much of Yosemite Valley to the west of Yosemite Village you must still use your car. Many of the park's most famous spots such as El Capitan, Bridalveil Fall, Tunnel View, Cathedral Rocks and Sentinel Rock are in west Valley locations. At least two resources are available for a "self-guided" circle tour. If you've got a cassette player in your car, try the *Yosemite Valley Tour—A Yosemite Audio Guide* by Bob Roney.

This audio tour is available for sale at the Visitor Center and at other park stores and is a comprehensive look at all aspects of the Valley—from geology to Native Americans to history to plants and animals. The sixty minute tape provides explicit directions to the ten stops on the tour which will take you from 2 to 4 hours.

An alternative is to use *The Yosemite Road Guide*, a well-written book which is keyed to roadside markers throughout Yosemite Valley and the rest of the park. You must develop your own route using the Road Guide, but it's packed with interesting information and facts which will enhance your tour.

If you would rather be free of your car and not drive, the YP&CCo. offers a two-hour guided tour in an open-air tram which visits most of the picturesque spots in Yosemite Valley. Check at the front desks of the various lodging facilities or behind the Village Store for tour details and prices.

Take a Bicycle Ride

Whether you've brought your bicycle or not, you can still see Yosemite Valley on two wheels. Bicycle rentals can be arranged at Yosemite Lodge (year round) and Curry Village (summer only) as can rentals of helmets and child carriers. More than eight miles of paved bicycle paths separate bicycle traffic from autos, and bicycling is especially good on the closed sections of roadway in the Valley's east end.

Try to avoid bicycling on busy Valley roads which are often flooded with automobiles. As a rule, distracted, sightseeing drivers are not particularly attentive to bicyclists. Apart from that there are some fairly strict rules for bicycle use in the Valley:

✻ Bicyclists should stay on paved bike paths and highways.

✻ No riding on trails and into meadows. Erosion and vegetation damage will result otherwise.

✻ Mountain and all terrain bicycles are permitted, but not allowed on unpaved surfaces in Yosemite Valley. Check at the Visitor Center for appropriate mountain bike routes.

✻ Ride to the right in single file.

Catch a Fish

There are lots of trout in Yosemite Valley, but the Merced River is heavily fished. Stocking of trout is no longer done, and resident lunkers have developed a wariness of people and their multifarious fishing devices. Nevertheless, nice fish are caught every season by anglers of every skill level.

Sport fishing regulations were adopted for Yosemite in 1990 that established a fishing season for streams and rivers in the park. Fishing is allowed in streams and rivers between the last Saturday in April and November 15 only. Fishing is still allowed year-round in park lakes and reservoirs. The daily bag possession limit is 5 per day and 10 in possession. California fishing licenses are required for all fisherpersons 16 years of age and over and may be purchased at the Sports Shop in Yosemite Village and at the Wawona store.

On the Merced River just outside the park between the boundary and downstream to the Foresta Bridge, fishing is allowed all year but only to persons using artificial lures with barbless hooks, with a minimum size limit of 12 inches total length and a maximum daily bag limit of 2. Consult the California Fish and Game Regulations for further Yosemite fishing rules.

Paint a Picture

Free outdoor art classes are available during most parts of the year at the Art Activity Center. Artists working in many different media offer hands-on learning experiences to interested students regardless of skill level. Located on the Village Mall between the U.S. Post Office and the Ansel Adams Gallery, the Art Activity Center is co-sponsored by the National Park Service, the Yosemite Association, and the Yosemite Park & Curry Co. Class sessions are four hours in length and are scheduled from early spring through October, and during holiday periods.

Ride 'Em Cowboy

Horseback rides are offered (for those with hardened backsides) by the Yosemite Park & Curry Co. from their stables in the east end of Yosemite Valley (bus stop #18). Guided trips in two-hour, half-day, and full-day lengths are given to such destinations as Nevada Fall and Glacier Point. For reservations call 372-1248. Children must be 7 years or older to participate, although walk-and-lead ponies and burros are also available by the hour. The stables are open from Easter to mid-October.

Get Your Head Wet

If you'd like to swim, the Merced River provides miles of beaches and numerous, refreshing swimming holes during the summer months (it's too cold and fast-flowing in the spring). Or try out Mirror Lake and Tenaya Creek. If you must swim in a heated pool, in summer there's one at Yosemite Lodge and another at Curry Village. A small pool is available for guests only at the Ahwahnee Hotel.

Indulge the Kids

The Happy Isles Family Nature Center is a great spot for parents and their children, open from early spring until October (check the *Yosemite Guide*). Here are exhibits of park animals, a children's corner, a night display and much more. Happy Isles is also the location for the Junior and Senior Ranger programs operated by the National Park Service each summer. Check with a ranger for details.

Go for a Hike

There's a price to be paid for Yosemite Valley's towering cliffs and sheer walls. Practically every hike leading out of Yosemite Valley is straight up and strenuous! But the Valley floor offers many enjoyable walks over flat terrain, and no matter what your hiking ability, you can find a trail to suit you.

When you hike be sure to wear sturdy, comfortable shoes and clothes which allow freedom of movement. Carry a flashlight and raingear. Rain (or snow) is a possibility in practically every season. Don't forget plenty of water (drinking from streams and rivers in Yosemite is not advised) and lunch or snacks. No dogs are allowed on the trails; please don't take short-cuts or ignore switchbacks.

Take in the Yosemite Theater

Throughout the year, dramatic, musical and cinematic performances are offered each evening through the Yosemite Theater program. Designed to supplement the interpretive activities of the NPS, Yosemite Theater is sponsored by the Yosemite Association which charges modest fees for the various presentations. Best known of the theater programs is Lee Stetson's one-man stage production in which he portrays John Muir entitled "Conversations with a Tramp." There's a program for every taste including "Yosemite By Song" (which will engage adult and child alike), the film *Yosemite: The Fate of Heaven* and others. Special "centennial" programs will be presented during 1990 and 1991 to celebrate the 100th anniversary of Yosemite as a national park. Tickets for the performances may be purchased in advance at the Visitor Center or at the door.

Hear a Lecture

Each summer the Sierra Club operates the LeConte Memorial Lodge, an educational center and library located across from Housekeeping Camp at shuttle bus stop #12. The lodge was built by the Club in 1903 in honor of Joseph LeConte, eminent University of California geologist. Berkeley architect John White designed the Tudor-style, rough-hewn granite building. Most evenings, special lectures are presented here free of charge to interested visitors and Sierra Club members. Consult the *Yosemite Guide* or visit the LeConte Lodge for a schedule.

Saunter in the Cemetery

Fascinating insights into Yosemite's history can be gained from a visit to Yosemite Valley's Pioneer Cemetery

Q: Where did the Mariposa Battalion camp on their first ever visit to Yosemite Valley in 1851?
A: In Bridalveil Meadow. There's a plaque commemorating this event on the edge of the meadow near the Merced River.

which is located across the street just west of the Yosemite Museum. Several significant figures from the park's past are buried here including a number of Native Americans. First laid out in the 1870s, the cemetery houses the graves of such persons as James Mason Hutchings, Galen Clark, James Lamon, Sally Ann Castagnetto, Suzie Sam and Lucy Brown. Guides to the Pioneer Cemetery can be borrowed at the Visitor Center desk. If you do visit the cemetery, remember that it is a sacred place for many and that proper respect should be shown.

Pack a Picnic

There are a number of fine spots for a picnic in Yosemite Valley. In the eastern end of the Valley, ride the shuttle bus to Happy Isles or take the walk to Mirror Lake. To the west try El Capitan picnic area (on the left side of Northside Drive, about a mile and a half beyond Yosemite Lodge), Devil's Elbow (about a half mile further where the Merced River makes a wide turn near the road), Bridal Veil Fall parking area (at the intersection of Highway 41 and Southside Drive), Cathedral picnic area (on the left side of Southside Drive just past the El Cap crossover), Sentinel Beach picnic area (on the left a mile or so further along Southside Drive), or Swinging Bridge picnic area (less than a half a mile further on the left). See the map on pages 22-23 for locations.

Take an Outdoor Class

Throughout the year, the Yosemite Association presents a series of outdoor seminars in Yosemite Valley and at other park locations. Many of the courses, which cover such topics as botany, geology, natural history, photography, art and backpacking, are offered for college credit. Programs have been designed for all levels of experience and for every type of Yosemite user including seniors and families. The instructional staff is excellent. For a catalog of classes or more information call (209) 379-2321 or write: Seminar Coordinator, Yosemite Association, PO Box 230, El Portal, CA 95318.

Three Easy Hikes on the Valley Floor

✲ **Mirror Lake.** Take the free shuttle bus to the Mirror Lake Junction (bus stop #17). During the winter you'll have to walk from the Pines Campgrounds (bus stop #19). From this point it's a relaxing half mile saunter over pavement to Mirror Lake. The hike around the lake is also gentle following Tenaya Creek eastward and then circling back. Walking around the lake adds about 3 miles to the total distance. Views of Half Dome, Mt. Watkins and Basket Dome are superb.

✲ **Vernal Fall Bridge.** This special vantage point is reached from Happy Isles which is stop #16 on the free shuttle bus route. (You'll need to walk from Curry Village during the winter when the shuttles don't stop here.) Undoubtedly the most popular and busiest hike in Yosemite (you'll be elbow to elbow with lots of other people), the Mist Trail leads seven tenths of a mile to a bridge which allows a breathtaking view of Vernal Fall. The trail, while paved with asphalt, is not as easy as the other two hikes listed here.

There is a moderate slope most of the way to the bridge, and a few ups and downs. But it's definitely worth the effort. If you're a strong hiker and still feeling hardy, the remaining hike to the top of the fall is about a half mile. Be warned, however, that it's all straight uphill over a very steep trail and a large number of granite steps. It's called the Mist Trail because it leads along the right flank of Vernal Fall which, particularly in spring, blows heavy mist over trail and hiker alike.

✲ **Lower Yosemite Fall.** Walk, drive, bicycle or ride the shuttle bus to the Lower Yosemite Fall parking area near Yosemite Lodge (bus stop #7). It's no more than a quarter mile to the base of the lower fall and its boisterous, watery display (at least most of the year). If you continue over the bridge and follow the trail, you will loop back to the parking area in less than a half mile. On full-moon nights in April and May, take this walk and watch for beautiful "moon bows" in the lower fall – a phenomenon first written about by John Muir. This, too, is a very popular excursion.

✲ **Note:** The floor of Yosemite Valley is crisscrossed with many trails, and paths hug the base of both the north and south Valley walls. From about any point, there's good hiking. Get out of your car and explore some of Yosemite's less-developed locales. You'll be amply rewarded for your effort.

Further Reading

✲ *Easy Day Hikes in Yosemite* by Deborah Durkee. Yosemite NP: Yosemite Association, 1985.

✲ *Map & Guide to Yosemite Valley* by Dean Shenk. San Francisco: Rufus Graphics, 1990.

✲ *Trails of Yosemite Valley Map* by Jane Gyer. Yosemite NP: Yosemite Association, 1987.

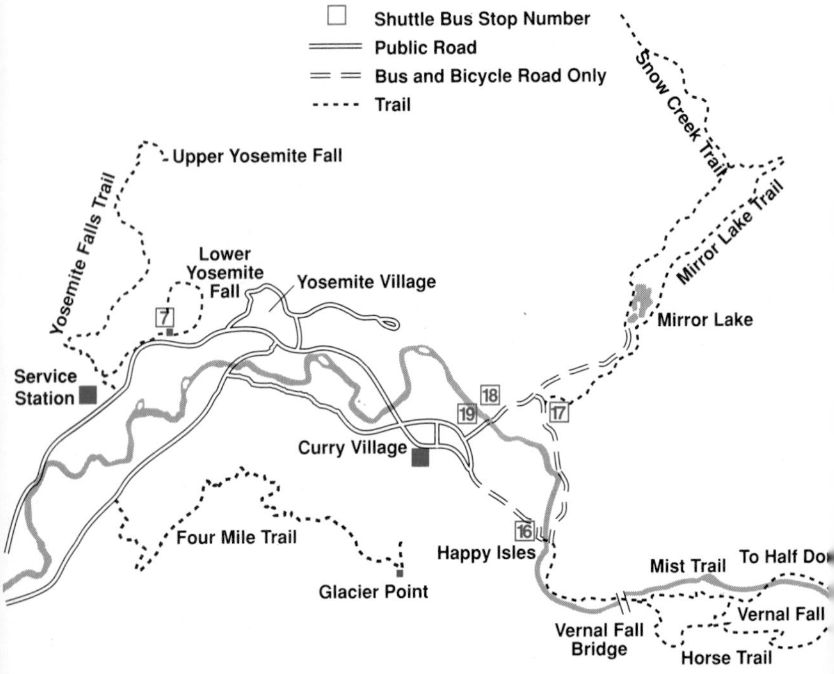

Four Classic Routes to Yosemite Valley's Rim

Each of the major trails to the Valley rim is very strenuous and consists of at least 3.5 miles of uphill over tens of switchbacks. Be sure you possess the requisite time, energy and physical condition before you set off on any of these hikes.

❊ **Yosemite Falls Trail.** This climb up the sheer north wall pays off with remarkable perspectives on both the Falls and Yosemite Valley generally. The trail leaves from behind the gas station across from Yosemite Lodge and next to Sunnyside Campground. The 3.6 mile route gains 2700 feet in elevation as it passes Columbia Point, the top of Lower Yosemite Fall and finally leads to the brink of Upper Yosemite Falls. When you reach the top, head back south toward the rim and find the walk down to the pipe railings. At this lookout, water leaps from the rock and braids itself into impressive patterns below you. Allow 6 to 8 hours for the round trip. Strong hikers should consider continuing on to Yosemite Point or Eagle Peak (see page 37).

❊ **The Four Mile Trail to Glacier Point.** Perhaps most disappointing to hikers on this route is that the Four Mile Trail is almost 5 miles long (maybe somebody rounded off a little too liberally). It's also an awful lot of work carrying yourself up 3200 feet only to be greeted by automobiles, lots of people and a snack bar at your destination. But the views from Glacier Point are sensational and all the more satisfying for the exertion. The trailhead is below Sentinel Rock on Southside Drive about a mile from Yosemite Village at road marker V18. To drive to it you must make a loop on the Valley's one way road system, crossing over at El Capitan (watch for signs returning you to Yosemite Village). One of the earliest trails built in the Valley, it is generally cooler than other routes to the rim given its location below and along the south wall. This hike requires from 6 to 8 hours up and back.

❊ **Half Dome: The Hike.** For many the summit of Half Dome represents a hiking challenge they can't resist. For all its allure, the trip is long (about 17 miles round trip), steep (4,900 feet of elevation gain), and physically demanding. It's rewarding, too, particularly the incredible views both along the way and at the top. The last 200 yards up the back of the dome require the use of steel cable handrails and will really make your adrenal gland active. If it sounds like too much of a grunt for one day, consider spending the night in Little Yosemite Valley (you'll need a wilderness permit) and make the ascent when you're fresh the next morning. This busy trail (someone estimated that about 600 people scale Half Dome daily during the summer) begins from Happy Isles (bus stop #16). Allow 10 to 12 hours minimum for the round trip.

❊ **Tenaya Zig Zags/Snow Creek Trail.** This is a less-used 3.5 mile route to the rim which actually originates in Tenaya Canyon, just east of Mirror Lake about 2.5 miles from shuttle stop #17. It affords stunning views of the Canyon including Clouds Rest and Quarter Dome, and directly across from you as you ascend, of Half Dome. Once you've hiked the 108 switchbacks to the rim, the closest promontory is North Dome which is another 3 miles (see page 37). If North Dome is your destination, allow 8 to 10 hours round trip. The trailhead is Mirror Lake which can be reached by taking a shuttle bus to the Mirror Lake junction (bus stop #17) and hiking half a mile to the east. From the lake the trail takes off to the north of the lake up the Canyon for a mile and a half, then turns left up the cliff.

❊ **Vernal and Nevada Falls Trails.** The walk to Vernal Fall over the Mist Trail is covered in the "Easy Hikes" section (page 30), but the trail continues on to Nevada Fall above. Describing the route is a bit difficult, because there are two different segments leading to the same place — one primarily for horses and one exclusively for people. The horse trail takes off just past the Vernal Fall Bridge and is less steep, though longer (3.5 miles to Nevada Fall). The Mist Trail (foot traffic only) continues on past the top of Vernal Fall about a mile and a half over switchbacks to the rim. Ascending a gully to its left, hikers are treated to the world-famous profile view of Nevada Fall. From the top of the fall, trails lead to Half Dome and Little Yosemite Valley, and to Glacier Point over the Panorama Cliffs trail. Depart from Happy Isles (bus stop #16) and give yourself 6 to 8 hours for the round trip.

Q: What was the preferred route of the Yosemite Indians to the north rim of Yosemite Valley?

A: They regularly used what we now call Indian Canyon, but no trail is maintained any longer up this very steep ravine.

Valley Camping

*Yosemite Valley for a home or camp,
the Grand Canyon for a spectacle.*
— John Burroughs

There are over 800 campsites in Yosemite Valley, most of them on the Ticketron reservation system year-round. Despite the fact that many of the campgrounds are practically void of vegetation and that campers are closely packed (population density in the campgrounds is higher than in Calcutta's most crowded neighborhoods), these campsites are immensely popular. After all, it's Yosemite Valley.

It was in response to this popularity that the strictly structured reservation system was developed. While the need to reserve in advance does discourage spontaneity and acting on impulse, it allows visitors coming from all over the US and the rest of the world to expect, with some certainty, that they will find a place to camp when they arrive. From all appearances and reports, the system works well.

As indicated above, the campground reservation system for Yosemite is administered by Ticketron, which has some fairly exact requirements. See page 12 for information on making a Ticketron reservation.

For campers without reservations who find themselves in Yosemite Valley, there is a Ticketron office at the north side of the parking area at Curry Village. Many times campsites become available due to cancellation, but to obtain one of them requires standing in line, sometimes for long periods of time. For information on the procedure, call the Yosemite Valley office at (209) 372-4472.

Camping Regulations

✳ **Camping Limits:** From June 1 through September 15, there is a seven day camping limit in Yosemite Valley. It extends to 30 days between September 16 and May 31. Thirty total camping days per calendar year are permitted in the park (the "no homesteading" rule). A maximum of six people is allowed in each campsite.

✳ **Check-Out Time:** Campsites must be vacated by 12 noon on the day of departure.

✳ **Bears:** Yosemite Valley and other park locations provide excellent bear habitat. Bears are attracted by the same foods many campers enjoy — marshmallows, hot dogs, watermelon, etc. You are foolish if you do not store your food properly in your campsite (it's also a federal law). Most of the Valley campgrounds feature bear-proof food lockers which are very effective. When a locker is not available, your food should be stored in odor-limiting containers and placed in your automobile's trunk. If your car is trunkless, tightly close all doors, vents and windows and cover the food containers with blankets, clothes or something similar.

✳ **Pets:** You may camp with your pets only in designated campgrounds. During the summer months in Yosemite Valley, the designated campground has been Upper Pines. Be sure to inform Ticketron when you make your reservation if you'll be bringing Fido or Garfield. Pets must be on leashes (no longer than six feet) at all times and are not permitted on trails.

✳ **Hook-Ups:** There are no recreational vehicle utility hookups in the park.

✳ **Firewood:** Collection of firewood of any kind in Yosemite Valley is strictly prohibited. This regulation is the first step towards eliminating campfires which have contributed significantly to serious air quality problems in the Valley. (It's also aimed at making people smell less smokey.) At this time, firewood may still be purchased from the concessioner. Please use established fire rings and grates. Use of chain saws is not permitted in the park.

✳ **Vehicle Parking:** All of your vehicles including tent and utility trailers must be parked on designated parking pads. You can't just drive into the middle of your campsite. If you have more vehicles than will fit in the allotted area at your site, you must park them elsewhere (i.e. Curry Village parking lot).

✳ **Dump Stations:** No wastewater of any kind should be drained onto the ground. That's gross. Use utility drains for wastewater and the dump stations at Upper Pines and Lower River campgrounds for other effluent.

✳ **Quiet Hours:** Campers are expected to maintain quiet between 10:00 pm and 6:00 am. Quiet generators may be used sparingly during the daytime, or not at all if I'm camped next to you.

✳ **Showers:** Try to stay clean during your visit. Unfortunately, there are no shower facilities in any park campgrounds. In Yosemite Valley showers are available for a fee at Curry Village and Housekeeping Camp.

Valley Campgrounds

The following campgrounds are located at an elevation of 4,000 feet in the eastern end of Yosemite Valley. Most require Ticketron reservations (see above) and have a nightly fee of $12 per site. Some creative person decided to include "river" or "pines" in the name of each campground, so be sure to take note of the location you've been asigned or you may spend hours trying to find your way home. As dates of operation are subject to variation, check with Ticketron or the NPS for details.

✻ **North Pines:** This set of 86 camp sites is located adjacent to the stables and next to the Merced River. Both recreational vehicles and tents are accommodated here between May and October. No pets are allowed.

✻ **Upper Pines:** The easternmost campground and the largest in Yosemite Valley, Upper Pines is closest to Happy Isles and the trail to Vernal and Nevada Falls. There are 240 sites here, and pets are permitted (the only campground where that is so in the Valley). Both RV's and tents are welcome, and a sanitary dump station is available. Open from March through November.

✻ **Lower Pines:** Across the river from North Pines with several campsites near the banks of the Merced. The 173 camp sites are available for both recreational vehicle users and traditional tent campers. Lower Pines is the designated winter campground and is open all year. No pets are allowed.

✻ **Upper River:** Located between Curry Village and Yosemite Village, this camping area is for tents only; no recreational vehicles are permitted. Many of the 124 sites are near the Merced River, and the campground is usually open from April through October. No pets are allowed.

✻ **Lower River:** Directly across from Upper River, this campground accommodates both tenters and recreational vehicle users (there's a sanitary dump station here, too). It features a number of desirable "river sites," but their location across the river from Housekeeping Camp makes for lots of congestion and noise. Normally open from April through November. No pets are allowed.

✻ **Sunnyside Walk-In:** This campground is primarily for climbers and backpackers; traditional family campers would feel out of place here. Climbing headquarters for Yosemite Valley, Sunnyside attracts mountaineers from all over the world. It's located across from Yosemite Lodge on Northside Drive just west of the gas station. Parking spaces are provided outside the camping area, and users must carry their equipment and food to their sites. The 38 camp sites are communal in nature; the daily fee is $2 per person. Operated on a first-come, first-served basis, Sunnyside is not on the Ticketron system. Open for walk-in campers all year around; no pets are allowed.

✻ **Backpackers Walk-In:** Designed for campers without vehicles, this area of 25 sites has no parking area. All access is by foot, and there's a two night maximum stay. Users should check in at North Pines Campground where a ranger will provide directions to the area. Open from May to October in a typical year. Campers are charged $2 per person per night on a first-come, first-served basis (Ticketron procedures do not apply). No pets are allowed.

✻ **Group Campground:** Special camp sites are available for organized groups in Yosemite Valley by prior arrangement; reservations must be made at least 12 weeks in advance with Ticketron. The fee is $34 per site for no fewer than 10 and no more than 30 people. Parking is provided for up to five vehicles per group, and all equipment and gear must be carried one-quarter mile to the campground. For information and reservations contact Ticketron at the address given on page 12. No pets are allowed.

Gas, Food and Lodging

Gas

There is a single Chevron gas station in Yosemite Valley which is located on Northside Drive across from the Yosemite Lodge. Major credit cards are accepted, propane is available, and it's open year around. Because it is the only gas station, things can get quite busy and you may have to wait to be served. In winter, it's a good place to have your tire chains installed if snowy roads make them necessary.

A repair garage is open all year in Yosemite Village behind the Village Store. A towing service is available 24 hours a day by calling 372-1221.

Food: Restaurants

Though the cuisine is strictly American and waits can be considerable during the summer, there are plenty of places to eat in Yosemite Valley. The following is a location-by-location listing of Valley eating establishments. Check the Yosemite Guide for hours of operation.

Yosemite Lodge

✳ **Cafeteria:** Open for breakfast, lunch and dinner the year round. Quick and perfect for families. Minimal waits when everything else at the Lodge is backed up. Inexpensive.*

✳ **Four Seasons Restaurant:** Serving breakfast and dinner the entire year. An attractive large room provides a more formal setting than the cafeteria. No reservations are accepted; you must appear in person and add your name to the waiting list. On weekends and holidays when the wait can be long consider eating very early or late if you prefer the Four Seasons. Inexpensive to moderate.

✳ **Mountain Room Broiler:** Offering dinner only, daily from spring to fall, and on weekends and holidays in winter. This is Yosemite's "steak house" featuring a mountain climbing motif. Check out the enormous photo mural. One of the only places to dine out-of-doors in the summer. No reservations taken here either, so get your name on the list early. Moderate to expensive.

Yosemite Village

✳ **Degnan's Deli:** Open year round for sandwiches, salads and picnic items. You can build your own sandwich and piece together a nice lunch basket. There's limited outdoor seating, so plan on making yours a moveable feast. Inexpensive.

✳ **Degnan's Fast Food:** Lunch and dinner selections, year around. Fare includes pizza, chicken, frozen yogurt and ice cream. Limited indoor seating, but a fairly large patio. Inexpensive.

✳ **The Loft Restaurant:** Serving lunch and dinner, spring to fall. The only sit-down full-service eatery at Degnan's (located upstairs at the east end of the building). A good variety of offerings, and a full bar on premises. Inexpensive to moderate.

✳ **The Village Grill:** Fast food breakfasts, lunches and dinners, spring to fall. Patterned roughly on a MacDonald's menu (look for the Royal Arches?), fare is primarily burgers, sandwiches and fries with a morning menu of breakfast sandwiches and entrees. Located next to the Village Store with outdoor seating only. Inexpensive.

Curry Village

✳ **Cafeteria:** For breakfast and dinner, spring to fall. Here is a cafeteria with style. The high-ceilinged dining area gives you the feeling of being in the mountains and is tastefully appointed (that's right, a cafeteria). A chuckwagon barbecue line is offered in summer. A family favorite with inexpensive prices.

✳ **Hamburger Deck:** Serving all three meals, spring to fall. This fast food outlet has about the same offerings as the Village Grill. Hamburgers to go for consumption on the deck outside. Inexpensive.

✳ **Pizza Patio:** Open daily from spring to fall. Pizza only served outdoors. Inexpensive.

The Ahwahnee

✳ **The Ahwahnee Dining Room:** Breakfast, lunch and dinner, year round. This regal dining room is a true delight. It's a joy to behold with its beamed ceilings and impressive chandeliers. Perhaps breakfast is the most enjoyable meal here; casual attire is allowed and one can experience a feeling of relaxation and elegance as daylight filters through the massive windows. Dinner is the traditional, formal meal at The Ahwahnee (though the views are obscured by darkness). Men must wear jackets with ties preferred, and reservations are required. Call (209) 372-1489. Moderate to expensive.

*Inexpensive: dinner for one adult might cost up to $10. Moderate: dinner for one adult might cost from $10 to $20. Expensive: dinner for one adult might cost over $20.

Food: Groceries

Yosemite Valley contains four outlets for groceries and camp supplies. They are open year-round with the exception of the Housekeeping Camp Store which closes in winter. Check the *Yosemite Guide* for hours of operation, or call the indicated phone number.

✻ **Village Store:** If you can't find it anywhere else in Yosemite Valley, come here. Of particular note are the butcher shop and the fresh produce. Located at the east end of the Village Mall at bus stop #3. Phone 372-1253.

✻ **Degnan's Delicatessen:** Included in the restaurant listings above, Degnan's Deli also has a decent selection of foodstuffs for picnicking and snacks. West of the Village Store and next to the U.S. Post Office on the mall. Phone 372-1454.

✻ **Curry Village Camp Store:** A general store with convenience items and gifts. Located in the Pavilion building next to the Hamburger Deck at Curry Village. Phone 372-1291.

✻ **Housekeeping Camp Store:** This is a convenience store catering to campers. It's open from spring to fall only. Located at Housekeeping Camp near shuttle bus stop #12. Phone 372-1432.

Lodging

The following is a list of lodging facilities, ranging from rustic to luxurious, existing in the Valley. Quoted rates are approximate only, based on double occupancy, vary with the seasons, and are subject to change.

To make a reservation for any of these overnight accommodations, see the information on page 11.

Yosemite Lodge

Open all year, the Lodge offers five types of rooms: deluxe rooms with balconies or patios (about $90), standard hotel rooms with bath (about $70), hotel rooms without bath (about $45), rustic cabins with bath (about $55), and rustic cabins without bath (about $40). All rooms and cabins without bath utilize communal bathrooms. Because of the removal of a large number of diseased trees, the without cabin area is both unattractive and hot in summer. Yosemite Lodge is preferred to Curry Village in winter because of its warmer location. The Lodge is situated near and offers pleasant views of Yosemite Falls and the Merced River.

Besides the restaurants listed above, the following are available at Yosemite Lodge: gift shops, cocktail lounge, post office, swimming pool, and bicycle rentals.

Curry Village

Open from spring to fall and on holidays and weekends in winter. Originally designed to provide an economical lodging alternative in Yosemite Valley, Curry Village still features the least expensive accommodations. They are of four types: hotel rooms with bath (about $70), cabins with bath (about $55), cabins without bath (about $40), and canvas tent cabins without bath (about $28). All cabins without bath utilize communal bathrooms. Located in the shadow of Glacier Point, Curry Village is cooler in summer than other Valley locations and is known for its informality. Nearby attractions are Happy Isles, the campgrounds, and the riding stables.

Other amenities at Curry Village are gift shops, showers, a mountaineering shop, a climbing school, swimming pool, and bicycle rentals. Curry restaurants are described above.

The Ahwahnee

Ansel Adams called The Ahwahnee "one of the world's distinctive resort hotels." Open year around, this grand and imposing hotel is definitely at the luxury end of the Yosemite lodging spectrum. Besides its regular rooms in the main building, The Ahwahnee features several cottages on the grounds. Rooms and cottages all have bathrooms and rent for approximately $195 per night. The Great Lounge is a study in high style, and the dining room (see above) is without parallel as an elegant setting for a meal. Located below the Royal Arches, The Ahwahnee offers fine views of Glacier Point and the Valley's south wall.

Other guest services available at The Ahwahnee are gift shops, a cocktail lounge and a swimming pool for guests of the hotel only.

Housekeeping Camp

The experience at Housekeeping Camp is somewhere between camping out and staying in a rustic cabin. Guests are provided a developed "campsite" which features a covered shelter, cots and a table. You must bring your own linen (or sleeping bags) and cookware. Call it luxury camping, if you prefer, which differs from staying in a Curry Village tent cabin because you are able to prepare your own meals. Each housekeeping unit rents for about $32, and the camp is open from spring through fall only. Housekeeping Camp is located near the public campgrounds and adjacent to the Merced River.

The camp offers public showers, a store, and a laundromat.

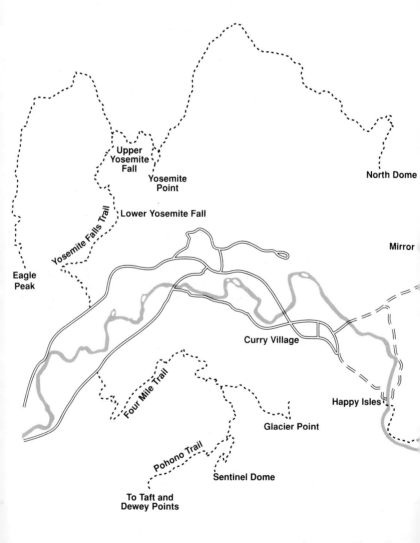

The Ten Best Views from Above

I can see for miles and miles. — Galen Clark

✳ **Glacier Point:** Not only does the point provide an overwhelming panorama, but it's accessible by car (for better or for worse). The commanding views of Yosemite's high country, Half Dome, Yosemite, Vernal and Nevada Falls, and the Valley below are unequaled.

✳ **North Dome:** This promontory allows the best view there is of Half Dome and Tenaya Canyon. Located on the north rim, it can be reached only by foot either from Yosemite Valley (via the Yosemite Falls or Snow Creek trails) or from the Tioga Road via the trailhead near Porcupine Flat Campground. All routes are very strenuous.

✳ **Eagle Peak:** This lookout is actually the highest rock of the Three Brothers formation. About three miles by trail from the top of Yosemite Falls, the peak offers impressive views of the entire Yosemite region, the Sierra foothills and the Coast Range far beyond.

✳ **Sentinel Dome:** Lacking Glacier Point's glimpses of Yosemite Valley, this dome is almost a thousand feet higher. An unobscured 360 degree vista presents itself to hikers who make the one mile walk from the Glacier Point Road. Particularly spectacular under a full moon.

✳ **Tunnel View:** While only part way up the southwestern rim of the Valley, this viewpoint just below the Wawona Tunnel on Highway 41 is a Yosemite classic. More film is used at this location than anywhere else in the park, and for good reason. El Capitan, Bridalveil Fall and Half Dome couldn't be more photogenic.

✳ **Half Dome:** The only drawback of a perch here is that the view doesn't include Half Dome! Something seems missing from the landscape when you're sitting on this enormous rock that has come to symbolize Yosemite more than any other landmark. The eight and a half mile hike from Happy Isles is quite difficult, though hundreds of people a day undertake it each summer.

✳ **Yosemite Point:** About three-quarters of a mile to the east of the top of Yosemite Falls, the point is famous for its proximity to the Lost Arrow Spire, a remarkable free-standing shaft of granite. The view to the south rim is one of the best.

✳ **Dewey Point:** The series of viewpoints along the Pohono Trail on the south rim of Yosemite Valley is special. Dewey Point can be reached from the trail that heads north from the Glacier Point Road near Bridalveil Creek Campground. Both Dewey and Crocker (a half mile to the west) Points allow unusual perspectives on El Capitan and Bridalveil Fall.

✳ **Rainbow View:** This location is about a mile and a half up the rockslides trail that crosses the base of El Capitan. While the hike is a rough one over boulders, from the viewpoint roughly opposite the east end of the Wawona Tunnel one is sometimes treated to rainbow displays in Bridalveil Fall during midafternoons in summer.

✳ **Taft Point and the Fissures:** Also on the Pohono Trail, these spots are accessed from the same trailhead on the Glacier Point Road that heads to Sentinel Dome. An easy walk leads to Taft Point with its view of the Cathedral Rocks and Spires and the north rim, and east to the Fissures which are deep clefts in the rock which drop hundreds of feet towards Yosemite Valley. Check out the echo here.

Half Dome Trail

Half Dome

John Muir Trail

Little Yosemite Valley

Fall

Mist Trail   Nevada Fall

══════ Public Road
═ ═ ═ Bus and Bicycle Road Only
- - - - - Trail

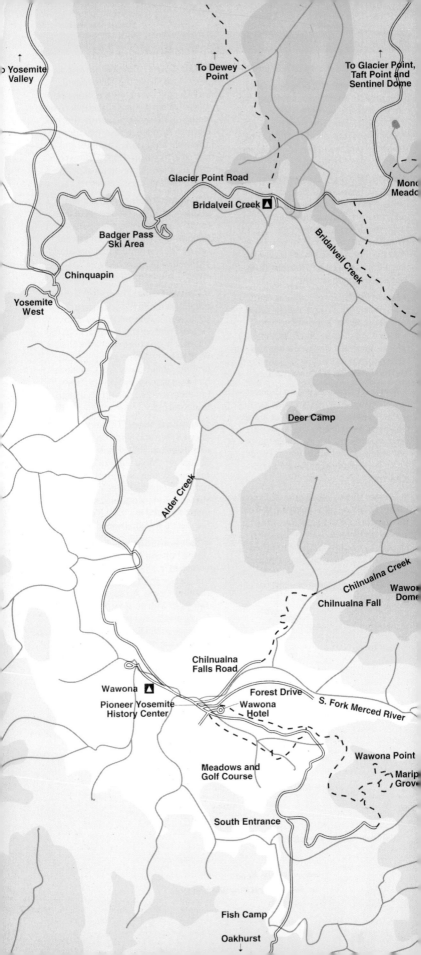

Wawona, Glacier Point & the Mariposa Big Trees

To the south of Yosemite Valley lies a part of the park which is less busy and noticeably quieter. Known as the "Wawona District," the south end includes the road to Glacier Point, historic Wawona, and the world famous Mariposa Grove of Giant Sequoias. All of these locations are reached by private automobile via Highway 41 as no shuttle transport or regular commercial bus service is available.

Mount Florence ▲

◪ Ostrander Ski Hut

Buena Vista Peak
▲

Crescent Lake

Johnson Lake

Buck Camp

Star Lakes

Mount Raymond

◪ Campground
Public Road
Closed Road
Trail

Wawona

*Wawona Meadows themselves might
be called the Sleepy Hollow of the West.
It is the most peaceful place that I know
in America, and comes near being the
most idyllic spot I have seen anywhere.*
— Joseph Smeaton Chase

Wawona is an historic community nestled on a beautiful meadow near the South Fork of the Merced River about 25 miles south of Yosemite Valley. The area was settled very early in the park's history and became a stopover point on the stagecoach route to the Park. Galen Clark, a significant figure in Yosemite's history (see page 101), built Clark's Station there, and that cabin later grew to become the Wawona Hotel we know today.

To the east of the main road on both sides of the river, a large number of private cabins and homes have been developed. This area, known as Section 35, was held privately for many years before it became part of Yosemite National Park. Known as an "inholding," the tract is still largely privately owned, although the National Park Service has purchased several homes and lots. Many of the residences are available as summer rentals (see the "Lodging" section below).

If you need information, directions or help, there is a ranger station in Wawona. To find it, turn off the Wawona Road to the east onto Chilnualna Falls Road. Drive approximately one quarter mile and turn right (just past the stable). Signs will direct you to the ranger station. The phone number at the Wawona Ranger Station is (209) 375-6391.

The Wawona Shuttle Bus

During the summer (as funds permit), a free shuttle bus operates in the Wawona area. Generally, the system runs from Memorial Day to Labor Day on a daily basis with stops at the Wawona Campground, the Wawona Store, South Entrance and the Mariposa Grove of Big Trees. Check the *Yosemite Guide* for details, hours and exact schedules.

Q: Name the three U.S. Presidents who have stayed at the Wawona Hotel.
A: James Garfield, Ulysses S. Grant and Rutherford Hayes.

Best Bets South of Yosemite Valley

✳ **The walk to Wawona Point.** Quiet, little-visited and offering a remarkable view, Wawona Point is the perfect destination for an excursion in the Mariposa Grove. See page 47.

✳ **The outdoor barbecue at the Wawona Hotel.** Enjoy a delicious meal on the lawn under the pine trees at this fine old hotel. Red-checked table cloths in the wilds. See page 50.

✳ **The ski slopes at Badger Pass.** Every winter, Badger Pass is transformed into a hot bed of skiing activity. Both down hill and cross country opportunities abound. See page 20.

✳ **Stage coach rides at the Pioneer History Center.** Hold on to your hat on this horse-drawn carriage as it makes a short loop to the Wawona Hotel. See page 42.

✳ **The view from Glacier Point.** From the railing at Glacier Point, you are lord (or lady) of all the Yosemite you survey. The view is unforgettable. See page 10.

✳ **A round at the Wawona Golf Course.** Play nine holes of this exceptionally scenic course or just take a walk once it has closed for the day. See page 42.

✳ **Ostrander Ski Hut in winter.** A nine mile ski from Badger Pass south of the Glacier Point Road, the hut offers shelter and warmth to backcountry skiers. See page 21.

✳ **The Wawona Meadow Loop hike.** Flat, easy and enjoyable, the hike circles the full extent of the Wawona Meadow. See page 43.

✳ **Old-Fashioned Christmas in Wawona.** Every year the interpretive rangers in Wawona put on a special holiday program including caroling, storytelling and tree-trimming. Consult the *Yosemite Guide* for details.

Public Road
----- Trail
Ⲡ Picnic Area

To Yosemite Valley

Chilnualna Falls Road

South Fork Merced

Stables

Wagon Shed

Pioneer Yosemite History Center

Store

Barn

Covered Bridge

Gas Station

Hill's Studio

Tioga Mine Equip.

Forest Drive

Pool

Chowchilla Mtn Road

Wawona Hotel

Hotel Annex

Golf Course

Highway 41 To Fresno

Activities at Wawona

Step Back in Time

The Pioneer Yosemite History Center is a collection of historic buildings which have been moved from other locations within the park. The center is located near the Wawona Hotel, just east of the gas station (prominent signs will direct you there). During the summer, park rangers and volunteers dress in period costume and populate the buildings. Each building represents a different time period in Yosemite's history, and the rangers engage in "living history," which means that they portray actual Yosemite residents from bygone days. You can try, but you'll have a hard time getting these old-timers to break character.

Interesting attractions are an exhibit of old horse-drawn vehicles, the covered bridge over the South Fork built in the 1870's that has been restored, and a blacksmith who actually practices his craft while you watch.

For a small fee, you can take a short ride on a horse-drawn carriage to get a feel for what early trips to Yosemite must have been like. During parts of the year, regular ranger-led tours of the History Center are scheduled (consult the *Yosemite Guide* for details).

Hit the Links

A conspicuous adjunct to the Wawona Hotel is its beautifully laid out golf course nearby. Whether you're a golfer or not, a stroll around the 9-hole circuit is both relaxing and replete with scenic vistas. (If you're a non-golfer, take your walk after the course is closed, please!)

The golf course was built in 1917 and features some of the most magnificent golfing holes anywhere. While the layout is not particularly long, it features lots of rough and water hazards, and is remarkably challenging. Watch out for deer grazing the fairways, particularly on the first hole.

Golf clubs and carts are available for rent at the Golf Shop, and reserving a tee time is recommended (phone (209) 375-6572).

Q: What was the toll to use the Mariposa trail through Wawona to Yosemite Valley during the 1850s?

A: Man and horse each way, $2.00; pack mule or horse, each way, $2.00; footman, $1.00.

Enjoy an Outdoor Barbecue

Every Saturday night during the summer, an old-fashioned barbecue is served outdoors on the expansive lawn of the Wawona Hotel. Red-checked table cloths sport steaks, hamburgers, corn on the cob, western beans and more. Check at the hotel desk for times and prices.

Get in the Swim

The South Fork of the Merced River as it runs through Wawona is dotted with swimming holes and beaches. Find a spot to put down your towel and cool off, or try your hand at fishing (see page 27 for general fishing information and regulations). Guests at the Wawona Hotel may use the small swimming pool on the grounds.

Horse Around a Little

A riding stable is maintained during the summer by the Yosemite Park & Curry Co. at the back side of the Pioneer Yosemite History Center on Chilnualna Falls Road (about 1/4 mile off the main highway). Guided horseback rides of varying lengths are offered. Stop by the stable for details or call (209) 375-6502.

Hike Some More

A variety of hiking awaits you at Wawona, from easy and flat to steep and strenuous. The hiking rules outlined for Yosemite Valley (see page 28) apply in Wawona as well. Give yourself plenty of time and don't undertake more than you're capable of.

Range with a Ranger

Throughout the year, a program of ranger naturalist activities is presented free of charge to the public in the Wawona area. That program is expanded greatly during the summer. Check the *Yosemite Guide* for listings and times.

Tour an Artist's Studio

The Thomas Hill Studio on the grounds of the Wawona Hotel is usually open in summer and features exhibits of the work of Hill along with other art programs. Thomas Hill used the building as a summer studio from 1885 until his death in 1908, and his fine landscape paintings of Yosemite and elsewhere have gained critical acclaim. Check the *Yosemite Guide* for hours of operation.

Three Hikes from Wawona

✲ **The Meadow Loop.** This pleasant walk begins directly across the Wawona Road from the entry road to the Wawona Hotel. Follow the gravel road about 50 yards across the golf course just into the trees and take the road which leads off to the left. This almost entirely flat route skirts the edge of the Wawona Meadow, then circles back, crosses the Wawona Road, and finishes up behind the Wawona Hotel. Approximately 3 miles total, the loop should take an hour and a half or less. The hike is easy, leisurely and picturesque.

✲ **Chilnualna Fall.** The trail to this delightful cascade is fairly strenuous, gaining almost 2,500 feet in approximately 4 miles. Start from the trail head, which is located 1.7 miles east of the main road on Chilnaulna Falls Road. There's parking space on the right for 25–30 cars. If the road turns to dirt, you've gone too far. The route is an enjoyable one through manzanita, deer brush and bear clover which finally meets with Chilnualna Creek. The fall, instead of leaping and free falling from some precipice, drops through a narrow chasm in a furious rush. Allow 6 to 8 hours for this 8 mile round trip. Carry lots of water in the summer when temperatures can be extreme.

✲ **Mariposa Big Trees.** Starting behind the Wawona Hotel is a long, uphill climb to the Mariposa Grove of Giant Sequoias. Primarily in forest most of the way, the trail offers excellent views of the Wawona Basin and Wawona Dome as it nears the big trees. The trail ends at the Mariposa Grove Museum in the Upper Grove near the fallen Tunnel Tree. Because the elevation gain is 3,000 feet in 6.5 miles, this hike is for the well-conditioned only. Figure on spending 8 to 10 hours making the up and back trip of 13 miles.

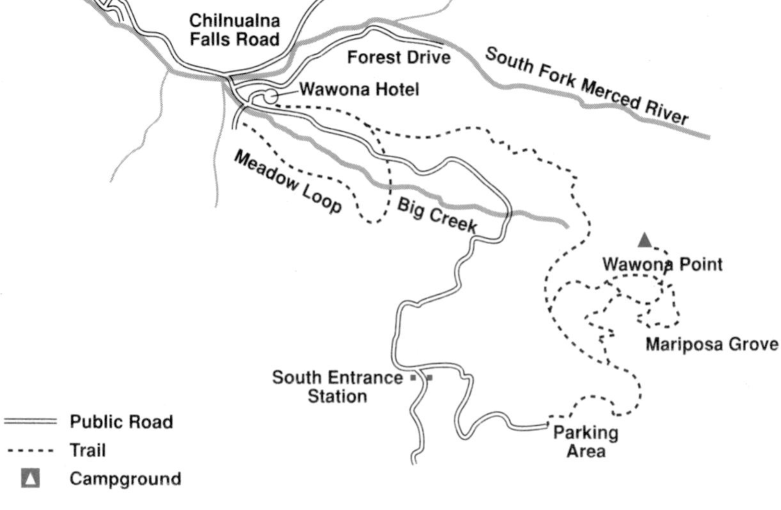

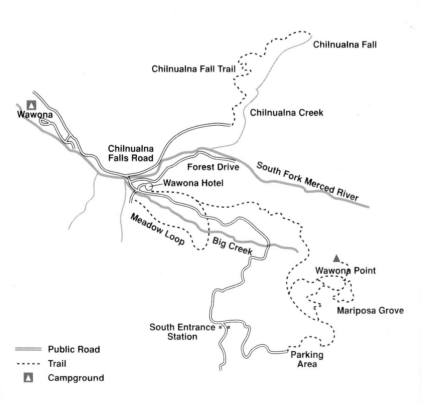

Activities Along the Glacier Point Road

The road to Glacier Point leaves the Wawona Road (Highway 41) at Chinquapin junction, 9 miles south of Yosemite Valley and 12 miles north of Wawona. The route winds 16 miles to the amazing promontory at Glacier Point, passing a variety of sites and attractions along the way, most of them short hikes from the road.

The route is open to the point during the three milder seasons, but in winter it is plowed of snow only as far as Badger Pass, the downhill ski area 6 miles from Chinquapin. Be sure to carry tire chains in your car if you're heading out the Glacier Point Road during the "off-season."

Q: Which landmark near the Glacier Point Road offers a 360 degree view of the park and is the location of a much-photographed Jeffrey Pine?
A: Sentinel Dome (the Jeffrey Pine has died recently).

Stare at the Stars

During the summer, ranger naturalists maintain a large telescope at Glacier Point and schedule regular evening programs which make use of it. There aren't many better spots for gazing at the heavens, plus you'll have the help of knowledgeable astronomers. Check the *Yosemite Guide* for dates and times and for the schedule of other ranger-led programs and hikes at Glacier Point and Bridalveil Campground.

Hike, Hike and More Hike

Given its proximity to the south rim of Yosemite Valley, the Glacier Point Road provides a series of natural trail heads for spectacular day hikes. And thanks to the YP&CCo., you have the option of walking all the way down to Yosemite Valley without needing to retrieve your car. During the summer, a "Hiker's Bus" is operated from the Valley to spots along the road all the way to Glacier Point. Call (209) 372-1240 for information.

Strap on Some Skis

Badger Pass, six miles from Chinquapin out the Glacier Point Road, is the center of Yosemite ski activity during the winter. Not only are there ski lifts, ski rentals and a lodge, but cross-country skiers are encouraged to utilize the groomed tracks out the Glacier Point Road (see page 20).

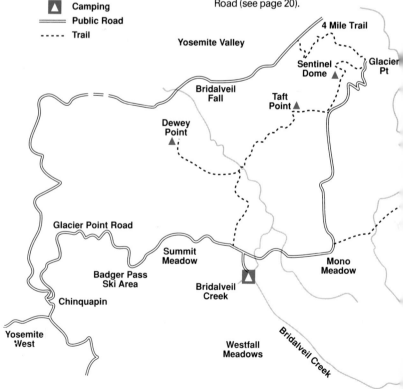

▲ Peaks
◪ Camping
═══ Public Road
- - - - Trail

Five Great Hikes from the Glacier Point Road

✳ **Dewey Point.** One of the most interesting perspectives on Bridalveil Fall and El Capitan is afforded by this commanding view point (7,385 feet). The trail starts two-tenths of a mile west of (before you get to) Bridalveil Campground on the Glacier Point Road. While there are trail markers on both sides of the road, you will want to head north. The route meanders through forest and meadows, intersects with the Pohono Trail (go left), then extends to the Valley rim. While there's not much elevation gain or loss, the round trip is approximately 7 miles. Allow 4 to 6 hours for the out and back hike.

✳ **Mono Meadow and Mt. Starr King View.** From the parking area 2 and a half miles beyond Bridalveil Campground on the Glacier Point Road, this trail leads to the east and to a terrific spot for admiring Mt. Starr King, Half Dome, and Clouds Rest. You will drop steeply for a half mile to Mono Meadow, then continue a mile further to an unmarked clearing where the view is an obvious one. Stop short of the switchbacks down to Illilouette Creek. The three mile round trip (a little strenuous on the way back) should take about 3 hours.

✳ **Taft Point.** Unusual rock formations and an overhanging lookout point reward hikers on this short route. Start at the parking lot on the Glacier Point Road about six miles past Bridalveil Campground (it's on the left, when you first catch a glimpse of Sentinel Dome). The trail is mostly flat and slightly downhill to the Fissures (wide gaps in the rock hundreds of feet deep) and Taft Point where you'll be standing on the only solid object between you and the Valley floor leagues below you. Be thorough in your investigation of the point which offers up several unique views. It's just over two miles round trip; give yourself two hours.

✳ **Sentinel Dome.** The trail heads for this hike and the one to Taft Point are the same. Park on the left about six miles past Bridalveil Campground on the Glacier Point Road (it's about at the spot where you first eye Sentinel Dome). The 1.1 mile hike to the top is a small price to pay for the 360 degree panorama of Yosemite's unbelievable landscape. You'll be at 8,122 feet (more than 4,000 feet above the Yosemite Valley floor); it's a good idea to have a park map for landmark identification. Try this easy hike at sunrise or sunset or on a full moon night. The round trip requires about two hours.

✳ **Yosemite Valley.** Take the "Hiker's Bus" (see page 44) or have someone shuttle you to Glacier Point and walk back down to Yosemite Valley over the Four Mile Trail (4.8 miles) or the Panorama Cliffs Trail via Nevada and Vernal Falls (8.5 miles). The Four Mile Trail begins to the left of Glacier Point and follows a series of switchbacks down the face of the south Valley wall. It terminates about a mile west of Yosemite Village on Southside Drive. The Panorama trail begins to the right of the Point, heading south to the top of Illilouette Fall, then back north and east to Nevada Fall (see page 25). There are two routes to the Valley (either the Horse Trail or the Mist Trail, see page 25) and trail's end at Happy Isles (shuttle bus stop #16). Figure on 3 to 4 hours to hike the Four Mile Trail and allow 6 to 8 hours to travel the Panorama Cliffs route.

Mount Starr King

▲

te Creek

Activities at the Mariposa Grove of Giant Sequoias

Located at the southernmost end of Yosemite, the Mariposa Grove is the largest stand of giant sequoias (*sequoiadendron gigantea*) in the park. These ancient monarchs are inadequately described with numbers, but how else do you do it? Some of the trees are 3,000 years old, others reach almost 300 feet into the sky, still others are more than 50 feet around. A typical mature sequoia weighs in at over 2 million pounds.

Notable trees here are the Grizzly Giant, almost three centuries old and 96 feet around at its base, the fallen Wawona Tunnel Tree through which a hole was cut and inside which thousands of automobiles and other vehicles were photographed before the tree toppled in 1969, and many others. There are over 500 sequoias here in two related groves, the Upper and Lower.

You may drive to the edge of the lower grove where hiking trails lead out among the trees, or open-air trams carry visitors throughout the area for a fee ($5.25 for adults and $4.00 for children and seniors in 1990). The trams cover a 5 mile loop which takes about 50 minutes if you don't get off to take a look around. The road to the Mariposa Grove is sometimes closed in winter when the snow is deep.

JANE GYER

Ride the Open-Air Tram

If you'd rather not hike into the Mariposa Grove, buy a ticket and board one of the open-air trams which will carry you out among these magnificent giants. They leave about every 20 minutes. The trip takes slightly less than an hour, but you'd be well-advised to get off the tram and spend a little time walking in the grove. The trams do not operate during the winter.

There are three regular stopping points along the tram route: the Grizzly Giant, the Wawona Tunnel Tree, and the Mariposa Grove Museum. On your way back down, consider getting off at the Grizzly Giant stop and walking the eight-tenths of a mile back to the parking lot. It's all downhill and remarkably relaxing.

Be sure to visit the Mariposa Grove Museum where there are exhibits about the giant sequoias, and books and other literature for sale. Restrooms are located there, too.

Walk in the Sequoia Forest

All trails into the Mariposa Grove of Giant Sequoias are uphill. From the trailhead at the far end of the parking lot, there is an elevation gain of about 1,000 feet to the Upper Grove where the Wawona Tunnel Tree is located, a distance of 2.5 miles. The going is gradual, however (22 children from Mrs. McDaniel's third grade class made it up and back!), and walking is the best way to appreciate the majesty and serenity of these stately trees. Be sure to check Park hiking regulations before you take off (see page 28).

Notable Sequoias of the Mariposa Grove

Name	Diameter at Base	Height
Grizzly Giant	31 ft.	209 ft.
California Tree	23 ft.	232 ft.
Faithful Couple	40 ft.	248 ft.
Columbia Tree	28 ft.	290 ft.
Clothespin Tree	22 ft.	266 ft.
General Grant Tree	29 ft.	290 ft.
Washington Tree	30 ft.	238 ft.
Lafayette Tree	31 ft.	267 ft.

Three Easier Hikes in the Mariposa Grove

✵ **The Grizzly Giant.** From the parking lot it's only eight-tenths of a mile and a 400 foot climb to the Grizzly Giant, the largest tree in the Mariposa Grove. Along the way you'll encounter lots of other sequoias and get a personal perspective on the mammoth scale of these trees. Allow from 1 to 2 hours for the round trip.

✵ **Wawona Point.** This excellent lookout on the entire Wawona basin is a short walk from the top of the Mariposa Grove. Get off the tram at the Wawona Tunnel Tree and walk back to the north to the Galen Clark Tree where the old road to Wawona Point branches off. Ask your tram driver for directions if you need them. The walk is only one-half mile and you'll be able to see back to the Wawona Meadow and golf course, with views to the east of Wawona Dome. The round trip walk should take you less than an hour.

Q: When did the Wawona Tunnel Tree fall over and why?

A: In 1969 as a result of the tunnel cut through its base, enormous impact to its root system from cars and people, and a heavy snow load.

✵ **Mariposa Grove Parking Lot from the Wawona Tunnel Tree.** It's always easier to hike downhill, so why not ride the tram to the top of the grove and get off at the Wawona Tunnel Tree. The hike down through the Upper and Lower Groves leads past the Mariposa Grove Museum and just about every significant sequoia in the area. It's only two and a half miles back to your car, and shouldn't require more than two to three hours to complete.

The Wawona Tree

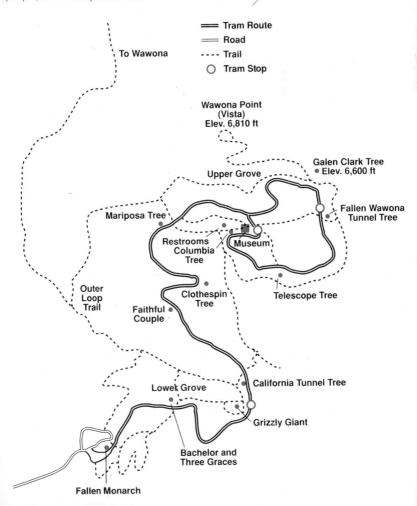

=== Tram Route
== Road
---- Trail
○ Tram Stop

To Wawona

Wawona Point
(Vista)
Elev. 6,810 ft

Galen Clark Tree
● Elev. 6,600 ft

Upper Grove

Fallen Wawona
Tunnel Tree

Mariposa Tree

Restrooms
Columbia
Tree

Museum

Telescope Tree

Outer
Loop
Trail

Clothespin
Tree

Faithful
Couple

California Tunnel Tree

Lower Grove

Grizzly Giant

Bachelor and
Three Graces

Fallen Monarch

Wawona History

The Wawona area was first settled by Yosemite pioneer Galen Clark (see page 101) who homesteaded 160 acres there in 1856. Though probably not deliberately, Clark selected a spot that was almost exactly half way between Mariposa and Yosemite on the route that developed for visitors. Clark seized the opportunity and built a rustic lodging house for travelers which was known as "Clark's Station."

Though Galen Clark recognized the potential of his way station, he proved unable to fulfill it. His management of Clark's Station was poor, and he invested considerable funds in completing the Mariposa stage road to Wawona. Financial pressure forced Clark to take on Edwin Moore as a full partner in 1869, and all signs indicated that Clark's fortunes had turned.

But over the next 5 years ill-advised investments in mining ventures and land purchases along with the completion of the Coulterville and Big Oak Flat Roads into Yosemite Valley spelled doom for Clark and Moore. They were forced to sell their lodging house and related properties to the Washburn Brothers in December of 1874.

The Washburns were an enterprising group of three brothers who came to California from Putney, Vermont. They undertook a number of ventures in the Mariposa area before purchasing Clark and Moore's. It was their New England background that led them to cover the existing bridge over the South Fork of the Merced; it's the same bridge that leads into the Pioneer Yosemite History Center today.

Contemporaneously with their acquisition of the Wawona traveler's stop, the Washburns began work on the completion of the stage road from Wawona to Yosemite Valley. In this way they hoped to compete with the other routes. They finished the job in June of 1875, and their plan began to meet with success.

In 1876 the Washburns put up the long white structure which stands just to the right of the main hotel building today. And when the main building burnt in 1878, the two story structure which is still known as the main hotel building went up the next year. Until 1882 the inn was known as Big Tree Station when it officially became the Wawona Hotel. Additional buildings went up over the years.

Congress established Yosemite National Park in 1890 and directed that the U.S. Army should be responsible for managing it. Because Yosemite Valley and the Mariposa Grove of Big Trees had already been granted to the State of California and were not part of the national park, locating park headquarters became a challenge. Because Wawona was one of the few developed areas within the new park (though not part of it) and for other reasons, it was selected as the summer command for Army personnel.

Known as Camp A. E. Wood, headquarters were located on the site of the present Wawona Campground. For 16 summers Cavalry troops from the San Francisco area occupied the camp and engaged in caring for the new park. Among their many activities were exploring and mapping, trail-building, fish planting, and enforcing anti-hunting and trespassing regulations. When the State Grant and Yosemite National Park were combined in 1906, Camp A. E. Wood was abandoned and Army headquarters established in Yosemite Valley.

Over the years changes to Wawona generally came with changes in transportation. With the completion of the Wawona Stage Road, the Washburn's stage company flourished and visitation grew. In 1914, automobiles first navigated the road between Wawona and Yosemite Valley. Wawona Hotel management determined that the automobile travelers preferred more recreational opportunities and proceeded to build a dance floor, soda fountain, croquet court, swimming tank and golf course over the next 15 years.

As the Wawona Hotel prospered, so did the community in Section 35 (the number assigned to the plot of land in its legal description) which included several homesteads and housed workers for the hotel and for other support services. When most of the Wawona region was added to Yosemite National Park in 1932, only Section 35 remained in private ownership. It is this area of Wawona where many private homes and visitor rentals are located today (see page 40).

Further Reading

✳ *Yosemite's Historic Wawona* by Shirley Sargent. Yosemite: Flying Spur Press, 1979.

✳ *Galen Clark: Yosemite Guardian* by *Shirley Sargent.* Yosemite: Flying Spur Press, 1981.

Camping South of Yosemite Valley

The campgrounds in this part of the park tend to be less busy and crowded, though in summer they are full practically every night. There is no advance reservation system for these campgrounds, and sites are allotted on a first-come, first-served basis. Because check out time is 12 noon, visitors would probably benefit by arriving by mid-day to arrange for a camping spot.

Camping regulations are roughly the same as those for Yosemite Valley (see page 32). Pets are allowed in designated sites in both the Wawona and Bridalveil Creek Campgrounds, and there are no showers in any Park campground. The camping limit is 14 days in summer south of Yosemite Valley, and a 30 day limit applies the rest of the year. A total of 30 camping days per calendar year is permitted in the Park.

✳ **Wawona Campground:** This popular spot is located at 4,000 feet in elevation on the banks of the South Fork of the Merced River approximately 25 miles south of Yosemite Valley on the Wawona Road. The daily fee for the 100 sites here is $7, and the campground is open all year (prepare for extreme cold and snow in the winter, however).

✳ **Bridalveil Creek Campground:** You'll find this group of 110 campsites 9 miles out the Glacier Point Road from Chinquapin (about 25 miles from Yosemite Valley). Open from June through September, the campground is much cooler than the Valley or Wawona given its location at over 7,000 feet. The nightly fee is $7.

✳ **Group Campgrounds:** Sections of the Wawona and Bridalveil Creek Campgrounds have been set aside for use by organized groups only. Arrangements must be made at least 12 weeks in advance, and special fees and regulations apply. For reservations and information, write Campground Supervisor, Wawona District, National Park Service, Wawona, CA 95389 or call (209) 375-6391.

Gas, Food and Lodging South of Yosemite Valley

Gas

The only gas station in this part of the park is located in Wawona, just north of the Wawona Hotel on the main highway. Major credit cards are accepted (it's a Chevron station), it's open year-round, and tire chains are available.

For towing services, call 372-1221 at any time of the day.

Food: Restaurants

For other than snacks and simple sandwiches, there's only one choice in the south end of the park—the Wawona Hotel Dining Room. If you're near the South Entrance, there are a number of good restaurants along Highway 41 between Fish Camp and Oakhurst, all within a half hour's drive. The following places to eat are open seasonally only; be sure to check the *Yosemite Guide* for dates and hours of operation.

✲ Wawona Hotel Dining Room: Serving breakfast, lunch and dinner from Easter week through October and on weekends and holidays in the fall. Located in the Victorian main building at the hotel, the dining room has retained an historic feel. The sepiatone photographs by Carleton Watkins and the sequoia cone light fixtures are perfect touches in this multi-windowed facility. The food is fine, the setting charming. If you're thirsty, the wine list is good and there's a full bar. Call 375-6556 for mandatory dinner reservations. Lunch and Sunday brunch are served buffet style. On Saturdays in summer try the outdoor barbecue on the Hotel lawn. Moderate to expensive prices.

✲ Wawona Golf Shop Snack Stand: Open spring through fall inside the golf shop at the Wawona Hotel. Cold drinks, hot dogs, prepackaged sandwiches, and other simple items are available if you're in a hurry or need a light meal or snack. Moderate prices.

✲ Glacier Point Snack Stand: A summer and fall operation with a limited menu. Primarily providing munchies for visitors to Glacier Point. Moderate prices.

Food: Groceries

Campers, vacation home renters and park visitors have two choices for groceries in the park south of Yosemite Valley. Check the *Yosemite Guide* for operating hours, or call the indicated numbers.

✲ Wawona Grocery Store: Located adjacent to the gas station just off the main highway and north of the Wawona Hotel. Phone 375-6574.

✲ The Pine Tree Market: You'll find this store in the heart of the community of North Wawona. It's less than a mile east of the main highway on Chilnualna Falls Road. Phone 375-6343.

*Inexpensive: dinner for one adult might cost up to $10. Moderate: dinner for one adult might cost from $10 to $20. Expensive: dinner for one adult might cost over $20.

Lodging

Wawona is the only area in the Park where the majority of the lodging facilities are not operated by the YP&CCo. The Wawona Hotel is part of the Curry system, and to reserve a room there, you should follow the steps which are detailed on page 11. You must contact each of the other lodging providers direct to reserve from them.

The quoted rates for the following listed lodging facilities are approximate only, based on double occupancy, vary with the seasons, and are subject to change.

Wawona Hotel

Open from Easter week through October and on weekends and holidays through Christmas. This is the oldest resort hotel in California; the structure to the right of the main hotel building was built in 1879. The white-washing, wide porches, well-kept grounds and an old-fashioned bathing tank (we call them swimming pools now) all suggest another era in Yosemite's history. It's a remarkably peaceful and relaxing setting, but guests should keep in mind that some of the rooms are 100 years old. Rooms with bath rent for about $80, while rooms which utilize a community bathroom are priced at about $60.

Besides a dining room (described above), the Wawona Hotel incorporates a golf course with pro shop and snack bar, tennis courts, and a cocktail lounge.

The Redwoods Guest Cottages

Open year around. This is a collection of privately owned vacation homes and cabins available for rental on a daily or weekly basis. Located in the privately held section of Wawona near the South Fork of the Merced (approximately 1 mile out Chilnualna Falls Road), the rentals vary in size from 1 to 5 bedrooms. The rates range between $62 and $100 for units which all have kitchens and fireplaces. For information call (209) 375-6666, or write to PO Box 2085, Wawona, CA 95389.

Camp Chilnualna Cabins

Open all year. Located on Chilnualna Falls Road on the north side of the South Fork of the Merced River (about 1/2 mile from the main highway), these cabins and vacation homes are a third alternative in Wawona. Most units have kitchens and fireplaces; rates vary from $55 to $150. For reservations or more information call (209) 375-6295. The address is PO Box 2095, Wawona, CA 95389.

Yosemite West Condominiums

Open year around. Just beyond the Park boundary, but accessible only via Park roads, these rental units are situated about half way between Yosemite Valley and Wawona. Their proximity (8 miles) to the Badger Pass ski area has made the condos a favorite of winter visitors. But cool summer temperatures and the short drive to Yosemite Valley (about half an hour) make Yosemite West popular other parts of the year, as well. Rates run from $69 to $95 depending on unit size. Information can be had by calling (209) 454-2033 or writing 5410 E. Home Ave, Fresno, CA 93727.

Yosemite West Cottages

Open all year. This collection of vacation rentals is not just limited to cottages. There are studio apartments, townhouses, log homes, chalets, A-frames and more. They are located just west of the park less than a mile south of Chinquapin off the Wawona Road. Only 15 miles from Yosemite Valley and 8 miles from Badger Pass. All units have televisions and kitchens. Rates range all the the way from $45 to $200 per night, and discounts are available for longer stays. For reservations, etc., call (209) 642-2211 or write PO Box 507, Bass Lake, CA 93604.

Q: What was the source of ice for the Wawona Hotel each winter from 1886 until 1934?
A: Ice was cut by hand at Stella Lake, which was created by damming and diverting the South Fork of the Merced River about a quarter mile upstream from the hotel. The lake froze to a depth of about six inches.

Q: What was the first public lodging house developed in the Wawona area?
A: Clark's Station, built by Galen Clark in 1856.

Hetch Hetchy, the Tioga Road and Tuolumne Meadows

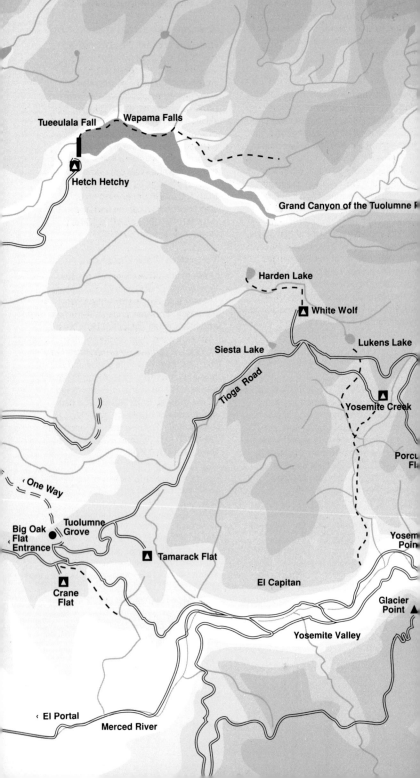

Tueeulala Fall

Wapama Falls

Hetch Hetchy

Grand Canyon of the Tuolumne R

Harden Lake

White Wolf

Lukens Lake

Siesta Lake

Tioga Road

Yosemite Creek

Porcu
Fla

One Way

Tuolumne
Grove

Big Oak
Flat
Entrance

Tamarack Flat

Crane
Flat

El Capitan

Yosem
Poin

Yosem
Poin

Glacier
Point

Yosemite Valley

El Portal

Merced River

*O*ver two-thirds of Yosemite National Park lie north of Yosemite Valley, much of that region being wilderness. The area is made accessible primarily by the Tioga Road, the only trans-Sierra crossing between Walker Pass in Kern County and Sonora Pass to the north. Spectacular high country terrain, brilliant blue lakes, and astounding granite peaks are reached via this route which leads through Tuolumne Meadows, the largest subalpine meadows in the Sierra Nevada. The road crests the range at 9,941 foot Tioga Pass.

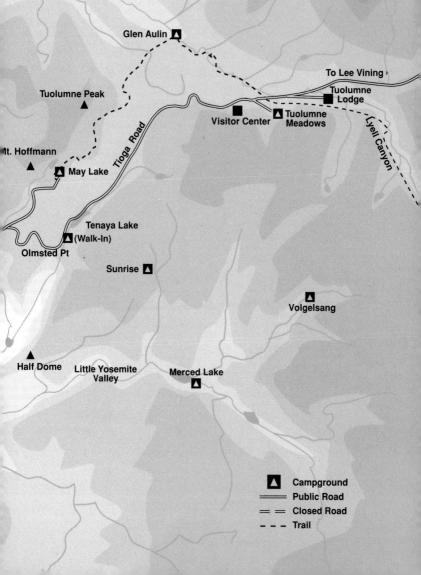

Glen Aulin

To Lee Vining

Tuolumne Peak ▲

Tuolumne Lodge

Visitor Center ▲ Tuolumne Meadows

Mt. Hoffmann ▲

Tioga Road

May Lake ▲

Lyell Canyon

Tenaya Lake ▲ (Walk-In)

Olmsted Pt

Sunrise ▲

Volgelsang ▲

Half Dome ▲

Little Yosemite Valley

Merced Lake ▲

▲ Campground
── Public Road
= = Closed Road
- - - Trail

Best Bets North of Yosemite Valley

✲ The summit of Mount Hoffmann. This is the geographic center of Yosemite, with extraordinary views in every direction. See page 61.

✲ The beach at Tenaya Lake. Unbelievably fine on a warm day, a terrific spot anytime. Enjoy a picnic, swim or simply take a nap. See page 59.

✲ The turnout at Olmsted Point. To see the vast expanse of glacier-carved granite is worth the stop alone. But there's much more, and marmots, too. See page 59.

✲ The hike to the Merced Grove. Flat, easy and quiet. Plus this is Yosemite's only sequoia grove where there are no automobiles. See page 56.

✲ A meal on the porch of White Wolf Lodge. Lunch and dinner are likely times to sit outside at this quaint spot and watch the White Wolf meadow do whatever meadows do. See page 68.

✲ A visit to Hetch Hetchy Reservoir. This body of water occupies a valley which has been characterized as Yosemite Valley's little brother. It has retained much of its beauty, and offers great hiking. See page 55.

✲ The trail into Lyell Canyon. The Lyell Fork of the Tuolumne River is one of the park's most peaceful and inspiring. The trail leads to and along it. See page 65.

✲ The High Sierra Camps. Whether you hike the full loop or just visit one of these five backcountry encampments, the experience will be unique. Stop for a mindblowing meal, or pamper yourself by staying over. See page 62.

WHITE WOLF LODGE

Hetch Hetchy

Whatever Hetch Hetchy means—grass, seeds, trees—it is no longer relevant; everything is covered by water.
— Peter Browning

The Hetch Hetchy area of Yosemite, as it is called in this book, includes the portion of the park which is found on the western boundary along the Big Oak Flat Road (Highway 120 West) north of Crane Flat, along the Tuolumne Grove Road between Crane Flat and Hodgdon Meadow, and along the Evergreen and Hetch Hetchy Roads (see map). The region is best known for its two groves of giant sequoias (the Merced and Tuolumne Groves), and for the Hetch Hetchy reservoir on the Tuolumne River.

National Park Service headquarters here are located at the Big Oak Flat Entrance (at the west gate of the park on Highway 120) which is home to a ranger station (phone 372-0350), a Ticketron reservations office, a small visitor center and book sales area, and public restrooms. If you've entered the park from the west over Highway 120, this is a good place to orient yourself; Yosemite Valley is still a 25 mile drive.

The route to Hetch Hetchy Reservoir is over Evergreen Road which is just north of the park on Highway 120 West. From the south, leave the park through the Big Oak Flat Entrance. The right turn onto Evergreen Road is one mile past the entrance station. From the north, turn left on Evergreen Road one mile before you reach the park on Highway 120 West. Hetch Hetchy is 16 miles out this road which becomes Hetch Hetchy Road at Camp Mather (bear right at the intersection).

Hetch Hetchy: The Dam

Many wonder how a facility like Hetch Hetchy Reservoir came to be sited within the boundaries of a national park. It wasn't easy or quick, but when the political struggle ended, the scenic qualities of Hetch Hetchy Valley had been "submerged" for the good of the citizens of San Francisco and their thirsts.

The city had been looking for a dependable mountain water supply, when shortly after the turn of the century, Hetch Hetchy was proposed as the perfect location for a dam site. The notion of a reservoir in Yosemite was not universally attractive, however, and John Muir, the Sierra Club and others opposed the project and fought it for many years. On several occasions the Hetch Hetchy project was outright rejected. But the city fathers were persistent, and in 1913, the Raker Bill granting San Francisco permission to dam the Tuolumne River at Hetch Hetchy was passed in Congress.

The loss of the fight to save Hetch Hetchy was devastating for Muir. Many believe that his efforts severely drained him, left him exhausted, and contributed greatly to his death about a year later. On the other hand, the reservoir proved an enormous success for the City of San Francisco which still relies on the project for the bulk of its water and power.

The dam was constructed beginning in 1919 and took about 4 years to finish. The resulting reservoir is 8 miles long, has a capacity of 117,400,000 gallons, and covers 1,861 surface acres (3 square miles). The dam itself is 410 feet high, 910 feet long, and 308 feet thick at its base which tapers to 24 feet at the top. One interesting fact about the Hetch Hetchy project is that the water in system pipelines flows all the way to San Francisco by gravity!

Activities in the Hetch Hetchy Area

The Hetch Hetchy area is best enjoyed in spring and fall, though it's remarkably mild some winters. The habitat of this region is more foothill than montane, and there are lots of Digger pines, manzanita and lower-elevation wildflowers. Stop at the Big Oak Flat Visitor Center (at the park entrance) to get oriented.

Walk Through the Big Trees

Yosemite's quietest stand of sequoias is the Merced Grove, accessible only on foot. It's a two mile hike into the grove from the trailhead on Highway 120 West (also called the Big Oak Flat Road). Located 3.5 miles north of Crane Flat or 4.5 miles south of the Big Oak Flat Entrance, the trailhead is marked by a post labeled B-10 and a road sign.

Follow the dirt road for about a mile, then take the left fork down into the grove. This is the park's smallest group of sequoias (about 20 trees) which was probably first discovered in 1833 by the Walker party. Look for the old Merced Grove cabin which was built as a retreat for the Park Superintendent, but is not used anymore.

These sequoias convey the silent majesty that has characterized them for thousands of years. The absence of motorized vehicles and the solitude are a real treat for hikers to the Merced Grove. Allow 3 hours for the 4 mile round trip.

Drive Through the Big Trees

If you'd rather not have to hike to see sequoias, try the Tuolumne Grove. A six mile one-way road leads through this group of 25 trees. The route is steep and narrow and not recommended for large recreational vehicles or trailers. An interesting attraction in the grove is the "Dead Giant" tree, a dead but still standing drive-through tree that was tunneled out in 1878.

The road to the Tuolumne Grove takes off near Crane Flat. From the intersection of Highway 120 West (the Big Oak Flat Road) and the Tioga Road (Highway 120 East), take the Tioga Road one mile to the east (towards Tuolumne Meadows). Turn left at road marker O–1 and follow the Tuolumne Grove Road a short distance to the first big trees. The road eventually passes by Hodgdon Meadow and meets the main road again at the Big Oak Flat Entrance. Turn left to return to Crane Flat (8 miles). There's a great picnic spot about a mile from the bottom on a small creek.

To avoid the 14 mile loop back to your starting point, leave your car at the turn-off and try hiking down into the sequoias. The round trip is no more than two miles and an easy adventure.

Let Them Entertain You

In summer, National Park Service rangers conduct a variety of walks, programs and campfires. Activities are centered at Crane Flat Campground and in the Tuolumne Grove, though other locales are used from time to time. Check the *Yosemite Guide* under "Crane Flat/Big Oak Flat Visitor Activities" for specific details and times.

Lookout for Fire

The Crane Flat Fire Lookout is staffed during the summer when the National Park Service watches the surrounding forests for signs of smoke. Visitors are welcome at the facility which is reached by a primitive road which leads off to the east less than one mile north of Crane Flat on Highway 120 West. The uphill trip to the lookout is one and a half miles.

Be sure to watch for fire and other emergency vehicles along the way. The view from the lookout is a special one with glimpses of the park in every direction. It's also fun to ski here in winter.

Q: Who was the first Euro-American to visit Hetch Hetchy Valley?
A: Joseph Screech in 1850.

Q: Where and when were the Big Trees discovered?
A: It is probable that the Walker party discovered the giant sequoias in either the Tuolumne or Merced Grove in 1833.

Hike Hetch Hetchy

Though the once beautiful valley of Hetch Hetchy is almost certainly lost forever, many of its scenic wonders can still be appreciated. Tueeulala and Wapama Falls still thunder from the north rim, Kolana Rock still rises imposingly from the reservoir's southern shore, and a remarkable variety of plant and animal life still populates the perimeter of the place.

While Hetch Hetchy is roughly the same elevation as Yosemite Valley, it's a much warmer spot. In the middle of summer it's downright hot. Perfect months for day hiking here are October through May. You'd be amazed at how warm the north side of the reservoir can be in the dead of winter.

The main trail at Hetch Hetchy leads over the top of the dam, through a tunnel, and along the north edge. The undulating route passes Tueeulala Fall, Wapama Falls (about two miles from the dam), and eventually Rancheria Falls (six and a half miles out). Hike as far or as little as you like. In spring, be prepared for high water and heavy mist at Wapama Falls which sometimes force closure of the trail. Retrace your steps back to the dam.

Fishing is allowed in Hetch Hetchy Reservoir, but swimming and boating are not.

▲ Peaks
◭ Camping
═ Public Road
----- Trail

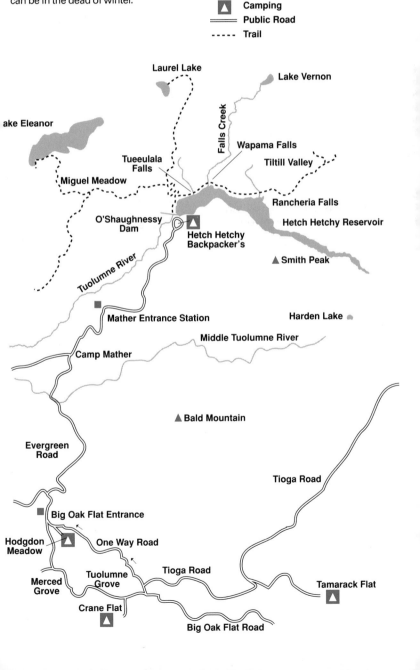

The Tioga Road

Originally a wagon road across Tioga Pass built by the Great Consolidated Silver Company in 1883, the Tioga Road literally splits Yosemite National Park in two. Improved to its present condition and alignment in 1961, the road opened up some of Yosemite's most stunning country and allowed access to previously remote high country destinations. Today the Tioga Road corridor is rife with scenic and recreational opportunities.

For the purposes of this book, the Tioga Road refers to the area of the park along the Tioga Road (which extends from Crane Flat to Tioga Pass some 46 miles east) except for the Tuolumne Meadows area. Visitors should be aware that the Tioga Road is not open all year. Heavy snows require the NPS to close the road (from November until May or June, usually), though snow is a possibility in any season; be sure to carry tire chains when driving this route in spring or fall. Typically mild summer weather attracts both recreationists and travelers headed east in large numbers.

There are plenty of options for fun along the road with multiple campgrounds, trailheads, lakes, streams and scenic views to choose from. If you need information or assistance, there are ranger stations at White Wolf and Tioga Pass Entrance (besides the Tuolumne Meadows Ranger Station mentioned below).

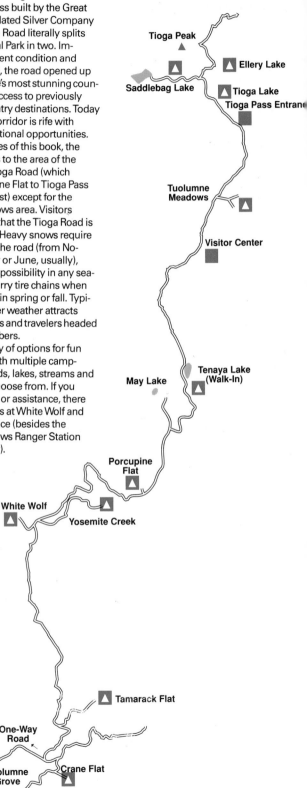

Tioga Peak

Ellery Lake

Saddlebag Lake

Tioga Lake

Tioga Pass Entrance

Tuolumne Meadows

Visitor Center

Tenaya Lake (Walk-In)

May Lake

Porcupine Flat

White Wolf

Yosemite Creek

Tamarack Flat

One-Way Road

Crane Flat

Tuolumne Grove

Merced Grove

Big Oak Flat Entrance

Hodgdon Meadow

▲ Peaks

◩ Camping

═══ Public Road

Activities Along the Tioga Road

Whether you're just passing through or making a leisurely trip along the Tioga Road, your experience will be a better one if you know where you are and what you're seeing. A valuable aid in this regard is *The Yosemite Road Guide,* an informative book keyed to markers along the way which is available at stores throughout the park or from the Yosemite Association. How else will you know about "Smoky Jack," the old Tioga Road, Siesta Lake and the ghost forest?

Get in Over Your Head

The best place to have a swim along the Tioga Road is Tenaya Lake. One of the park's larger lakes, Tenaya is approximately 8 miles east of Tuolumne Meadows, or 30 miles east of Crane Flat. The inviting sandy beach on the eastern shore is a good bet, but be prepared for some cold water. Tenaya Lake is also a favorite of sailboarders, windsurfers and sailboaters (check with a ranger for regulations). Use the dressing and bathrooms in the parking lot just east of the lake. If it's too cold to swim, have a picnic in this dramatic setting.

Be Programmed

During summer, ranger-naturalists offer free programs for visitors at various locations along the Tioga Road. Likely meeting places are White Wolf and Tenaya Lake, but check the *Yosemite Guide* for details.

Travel on Four Feet

Take a horseback ride from the stable at White Wolf. Turn off the Tioga Road about 15 miles east of Crane Flat and follow the road one mile or so to White Wolf Lodge. The stable is immediately behind the lodge and offers guided 2-hour, half-day and all-day rides. Plus walk and lead burros and ponies are available. Call 372-1323 for more information.

Q: How did Gin Flat (about 5 miles west of Crane Flat on the Tioga Road) get its name?
A: Reportedly, a barrel of gin fell off a freight wagon, unmissed by the driver. It was found by a bunch of cowboys, sheepherders, and roadworkers who got "ginned up."

Hike All You Like

The Tioga Road is a veritable hiker's wonderland. From numerous points along the route trails lead into a landscape unequalled anywhere in the world. Hikes range from easy to very strenuous, and become more difficult with the increased elevation. Follow basic hiking precautions (see page 28), and in this high country setting, stay hydrated by drinking lots of liquids. The most common hiking-related ailment is altitude sickness; consider spending a day or so getting acclimatized before starting to hike.

For those hikers who travel to Yosemite without a car or who wish to leave their vehicle in Yosemite Valley, there's a hiker's bus operated by the YP&CCo., which crosses the Tioga Road each day from July 1 to Labor Day. You can arrange to get off at trailheads along the way. The bus returns to Yosemite Valley every afternoon. For information, call (209) 372-1240.

Wet A Line

Fishing can be amazingly good along the Tioga Road. Spots like Lukens Lake, Harden Lake, Tenaya Lake and May Lake (all described above) are home to many feisty, if somewhat small, trout. Yosemite Creek and the Dana Fork of the Tuolumne River can also yield up a fish or two. The general park fishing regulations apply (see page 27); check with a park ranger for any special rules.

Check Out Half Dome's Back Side

One of Yosemite's most remarkable scenic overlooks is found at Olmsted Point which shouldn't be missed. This major pullout is located at road marker T–24 which is 2 and a half miles west of Tenaya Lake and just slightly more than 2 miles east of the May Lake turnoff. Here the enormity of the granite walls of Tenaya Canyon is revealed and unique views of Half Dome and Clouds Rest are allowed. To the east, the landscape includes Tenaya Lake and the many domes and peaks of the Tuolumne Meadows region. A short nature trail leads down from the point, and watch for fat and sassy marmots in the rocks (but please don't feed them).

Seven Sensational Hikes From the Tioga Road

✲ **1. Harden Lake.** This is a relatively flat three-mile walk to an attractive little lake which offers picnicking, swimming and fishing. Start in front of the White Wolf Campground and head north on what was the original Tioga Road. You can follow the road all the way to the lake or catch a trail which branches off about a mile from it. If you take the road, bear to the right when it branches. There's a good view of the Tuolumne River Canyon from the far side of the lake. The round trip is about 6 miles and should take about 4 hours.

✲ **2. Lukens Lake.** It's mostly uphill, but this hike of less than a mile terminates at a lovely spot amid meadow flowers and grasses. Being so close to the road, Lukens Lake is perfect for families with young (but not infant) children. Take your fishing poles and a picnic lunch. The trailhead is found 1.8 miles to the east of the White Wolf intersection; it's also 3 miles west of the spot where the Tioga Road crosses Yosemite Creek. Head north up the hill, then drop down to the lake. This easy hike is not quite two miles up and back, and requires about an hour to cover (a little longer for families!).

✲ **3. Yosemite Creek to Yosemite Valley.** From the point on the Tioga Road where it crosses Yosemite Creek (about 5 miles east of the White Wolf junction), a trail leads southward over level and downhill terrain all the way to Yosemite Valley. Because it's a one-way hike of 13 miles, you'll have to arrange for a ride to the trailhead, plan on shuttling back to pick up your car on the Tioga Road, or use the "Hiker's Bus" mentioned above. The trail follows Yosemite Creek down to Yosemite Creek Campground and eventually to the top of Yosemite Falls. Check out the spectacular view from the top (see page 31) before descending the final three and a half miles to the Yosemite Valley floor. This is a strenuous hike for the physically fit. Allow at least 8 hours for this demanding but satisfying trip.

✲ **4. North Dome.** This difficult hike to one of the best views of Yosemite Valley (see page 37) takes off to the south of the Tioga Road at road marker T–19, about 5 miles beyond the point where the road crosses Yosemite Creek (this is also 2 miles west of the May Lake turn-off and just east of Porcupine Flat Campground). The walk is mostly downhill and flat for 4.2 miles to the dome. Watch for the erratic boulders left by the glaciers here, and check out the impressive view of Half Dome directly across from you. Because the return trip to the Tioga Road is mostly uphill, this should be considered a strenuous hike. Give yourself 6 to 8 hours for the 8 and a half mile trip out and back.

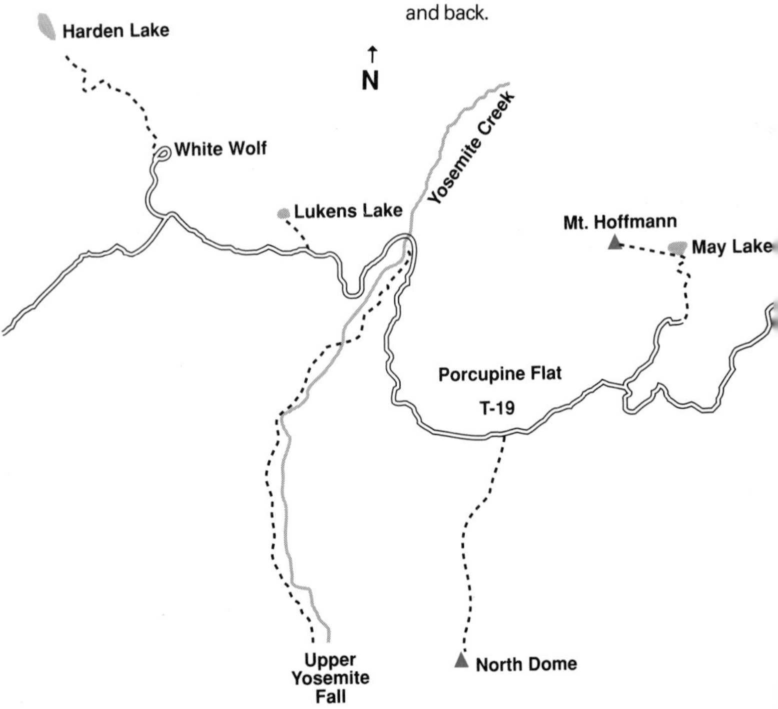

✳ 5. May Lake and Mount Hoffmann.

For those who like to get in the middle of things, Mount Hoffmann is the geographic center of Yosemite National Park. It offers superb views of the park's high country from its 10,850 foot summit. The trail up the mountain leads past idyllic May Lake, a beautiful spot and location of one of the High Sierra Camps (see page 62). Start your hike at the May Lake parking area. Turn north off the Tioga Road about 5 miles west of Tenaya Lake at road marker T–21 and drive 2 miles to the parking lot. It's an easy mile and a quarter trip to May Lake, and if you're adventurous, the 2 miles beyond to the top of Mount Hoffmann are considerably more strenuous (you will gain about 1,500 feet in elevation). Plan on 2 hours round trip for May Lake, and add 3 to 4 more for the ascent of Mount Hoffmann.

✳ 6. Mono Pass.

This high elevation hike is a comparatively easy four miles with an elevation gain of only 1,000 feet. The route, however, begins at nearly 10,000 feet and almost reaches the 11,000 foot level (prepare for some heavy breathing). The trail begins 2 miles west of Tioga Pass at road marker T–35, and heads south along an old Indian trading route. At Mono Pass itself are the remains of several mining buildings and cabins which were used during the late 1800's. Views of Mt. Gibbs and Mt. Dana are extremely fine. This 8 mile round trip should take from 4 to 6 hours depending upon your level of conditioning.

✳ 7. Gaylor Lakes.

Here's another trip for high elevation freaks who love to huff and puff. The trail ascends steeply to the north from just a few feet west of the Tioga Pass Entrance Station which is 9,945 feet high. Middle Gaylor Lake is about a mile from the trailhead, but it's no easy climb. Follow the inflowing creek to Upper Gaylor Lake and the remnants of a stone shelter at the Great Sierra Mine 300 yards to its north. This is truly an alpine environment with few trees, strong winds and often harsh weather. Allow 3 hours for this moderately difficult hike of 4 miles round trip.

Q: How should a hiker behave in a lightning storm?

A: Stay clear of open expanses of water, keep off open areas of rock and out of meadows, and stay away from prominent landmarks like lone, isolated trees. Seek shelter from the storm; a dense stand of trees of roughly the same height works well.

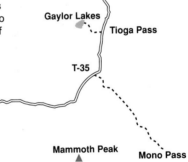

Gaylor Lakes

Tioga Pass

T-35

Tuolumne Meadows

Mammoth Peak ▲

Mono Pass

Lake

===== **Public Road**
- - - - - **Trail**

The High Sierra Camps

Six rustic colonies of tents in the park's loftier regions constitute an institution unique to Yosemite called the High Sierra Camps. Placed in a roughly circular pattern about one day's hike apart, the camps allow visitors to enjoy high elevation backcountry in semi-luxury. The semi-luxury aspect of the operation consists of wholesome hot meals prepared by the camp staff, and the regulation beds with mattresses (featuring sheets and down comforters) that await weary travelers. There are even showers!

The idea for the camps was that of Washington B. Lewis, Yosemite's first NPS Superintendent. He wanted hikers to enjoy Yosemite's high country free from the "irksome" load of equipment and food normally needed for a backcountry trip. In 1924, the first camps were installed at a number of locations (several of which already had unofficial "High Sierra Camps") and the system was underway.

Over the years there have been as many as eight different camp sites (including Little Yosemite Valley, Boothe Lake, Lyell Canyon and Tenaya Lake), but the present configuration of six has been set for quite some time. The camps are open for a very short season (roughly late June to Labor Day), and are operated by YP&CCo.

The only camp accessible by road is the Tuolumne Lodge (see page 68). Many people use it as a starting or ending point for the High Sierra Loop Trip. In a clockwise direction from Tuolumne Meadows, the other camps are Vogelsang, Merced Lake, Sunrise, May Lake and Glen Aulin. Each is located in an area of particular scenic beauty or with special recreational opportunities. The distance between each averages nine miles.

Guests at the High Sierra Camps are accommodated in dormitory-style tents which sleep either four or six. The communal bathhouses offer running water, showers and toilets. Hearty breakfasts and dinners are served daily, and bag lunches can be ordered. Size of the camps vary, but about 50 people on average can be lodged. Sometimes non-camp hikers can buy a meal in the camp dining tent which is an enormous treat if you've been eating dehydrated food for a week. Try making a meal reservation in advance by calling the number below, or check at the registration counter for availability.

A favorite of many High Sierra Camp users is the 7-day guided loop trip. A maximum of 20 persons are accompanied by a naturalist who provides ongoing interpretation of the geology and natural history of Yosemite's backcountry. Campfire programs occur nightly, and members of the group develop a real spirit of camaraderie and friendship.

If you hadn't already figured it out, the High Sierra Camps are tremendously popular. Despite the price, which is relatively steep, the camps are completely booked almost every night of the summer. Reservations are essential and are handled on a first-come, first-served basis beginning on the first Monday of each December for the following season. For information write to the High Sierra Desk, Yosemite Reservations, 5410 E. Home Avenue, Fresno, CA 93727 or call (209) 454-2022.

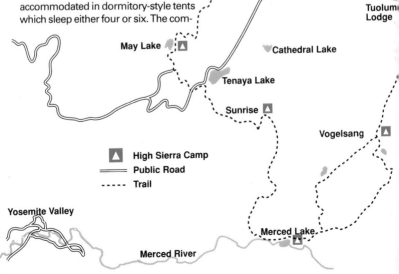

Glen Aulin

Tuolumne River

Tuolumne M

Tuolumne Lodge

May Lake

Cathedral Lake

Tenaya Lake

Sunrise

Vogelsang

▲ High Sierra Camp
═══ Public Road
- - - - Trail

Yosemite Valley

Merced Lake

Merced River

Tuolumne Meadows

The Tuolumne Meadow is a beautiful grassy plain of great extent, thickly enameled with flowers, and surrounded with the most magnificent scenery.
—*Joseph LeConte*

This stunningly picturesque region sits 8,600 feet up in the transparent sky of Yosemite's high country. Contained in a basin about 2 and a half miles long, the meadow system may be the largest in the Sierra Nevada at the subalpine level. Tuolumne Meadows is only 55 miles by road from Yosemite Valley, but it's a world apart.

Called by some the "hub" or "heart" of the high country, Tuolumne is a seasonal phenomenon. It is closed by snow to visitation the bulk of year, but when summer comes, the action begins. Hikers flock here, both daytrippers and backpackers. Rockclimbers who winter in Yosemite Valley adopt Tuolumne as a summer home. And visitors in their cars arrive to revel in the awesome beauty of the place, and to enjoy a less developed part of the park.

There's plenty to gawk at, too. The Tuolumne River winds its way sinuously through the meadows, while an array of unusually-shaped domes rings the area. There are smooth-bottomed canyons and jagged peaks; delicate lakes and odorous springs. These multiple elements combine to create a landscape both wonderful and inspiring.

During the summer months there's a ranger station at Tuolumne Meadows operated by the National Park Service along with a small visitor's center. The ranger station is just off the Tioga Road along the road to Tuolumne Lodge, and the Visitor's Center is located at about the half way point of the meadows about a quarter mile west of the gas station and store. For information or assistance call 372-0263 or 372-0450.

Q: What are the small chipmunk-like creatures that are seen everywhere in the Tuolumne area?
A: They are Belding ground squirrels, also known as "Picket Pins" for their habit of standing up straight like small stakes.

Q: What is the final destination of the water in the Tuolumne River that flows through Tuolumne Meadows?
A: The water is captured at Hetch Hetchy Reservoir and eventually ends up in the domestic water system of the City of San Francisco.

↑
N

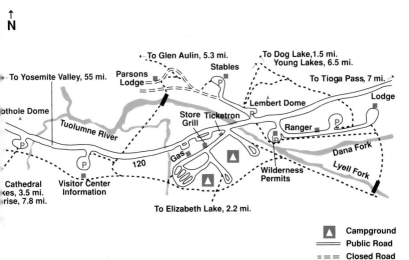

▲	Campground
═══	Public Road
= = =	Closed Road
· - - - ·	Trail
P	Parking

Activities at Tuolumne

Climb A Dome

Scrambling to the top of one of Tuolumne's granite domes can be fun and exhilarating. It can also be hazardous to your health. Try one of the easier rocks like Lembert Dome (see the hiking section below) or Pothole Dome (adjacent to the road at the west end of the meadows). Wear proper footwear and don't go up anything you aren't sure you can get down. Climbing lessons are available from the Mountaineering School in Tuolumne Meadows. Call (209) 372-1244 for details and rates.

Take A Swim

Because they are fed by the melting snow nearby, most of the streams, rivers and lakes of the Tuolumne region are freezing cold. As the summer progresses, they warm a bit, but swimming is not for the weak of heart. There are plenty of good swimming holes along the Tuolumne River as it passes the campground, and on its fork that passes lazily through Lyell Canyon (see hiking section below). Lake swimmers should try Tenaya Lake 7 miles to the west, Elizabeth Lake or Dog Lake (both described below).

Become A Sheepwatcher

In 1986, a small herd of California bighorn sheep were transplanted to the park in the Tioga Pass region. The sheep are native to the park, but by way of disease and hunting they were eliminated here before 1900. In recent summers there have been reports of bighorn sightings in the Tuolumne Meadows area. Check at the Visitor's Center for information and directions.

Get Tall in the Saddle

Riding horses are stabled at Tuolumne Meadows by the YP&CCo. As is the case throughout the park, they offer 2-hour, half-day and all-day guided horseback trips. The Tuolumne stable can be found by turning north at road marker T–32 which is just east of the bridge over the Tuolumne River near the campground. If you've got children, walk and lead ponies and burros can be rented. For more information and rates, call (209) 372-1327.

Walk A Mile in Your Shoes

The hiking around Tuolumne Meadows is first-rate. The trails are varied, the scenery is exceptional, and the weather usually cooperative (but plan for afternoon thundershowers, particularly in August). A person staying at Tuolumne could take a different hike every day for a week and still not exhaust the possibilities. Be sure to follow normal hiking precautions (see page 28) and drink extra liquids to keep yourself hydrated at this high elevation.

The YP&CCo. hiker's bus visits Tuolumne Meadows once a day from July 1 through Labor Day. You can be dropped off at the trailhead of your choice and, if the timing works out, be picked up later. Call (209) 372-1240 for information.

A great map and guide to hiking in the Tuolumne Meadows area is called *Guide to Yosemite High Sierra Trails* and is available at Visitor Centers and stores or from the Yosemite Association.

Get Centered

To learn more about the Tuolumne Meadows region, visit the Visitor Center located south of the Tioga Road a short ways west of the gas station. There you'll find exhibits, knowledgeable rangers, and books and maps for sale. It's also a good place to find out about free ranger walks and programs that will be happening during your visit (or check the *Yosemite Guide*).

During the summer, there is usually a Junior Ranger program for children with opportunities for them to earn a Junior Ranger certificate and learn lots more about the park. Check at the Visitor Center for information about the program, or call 372-0263.

Do Something Fishy

Tuolumne Meadows is loaded with family fishing opportunities. These high country trout seem to be plentiful and small. Your kids will find the many rivers and lakes great places to practice their angling techniques. The Tuolumne River and its tributaries are excellent spots as are Dog Lake, Cathedral Lake and Elizabeth Lake. Follow park fishing regulations (see page 27), and check at the Visitor Center for information or tips.

Seven Scintillating Hikes from Tuolumne Meadows

❋ **1. Cathedral Lakes.** Taking off from the obvious parking lot at the west end of Tuolumne Meadows (south of the road), this trail is fairly strenuous gaining about 1,000 feet in under 4 miles. The route is uphill, then relatively flat for a ways, then uphill again before it drops into the Cathedral Lakes basin. Watch for the right fork in the trail to reach the lower lake which is the larger of the two. Take a swim, enjoy your lunch, or fish a little. Your view of Cathedral Peak will be outstanding. The round trip is less than 8 miles and should take 4 to 6 hours.

❋ **2. Elizabeth Lake.** It's steep and short and well worth the effort. Elizabeth Lake is a lovely spot nestled against the base of Unicorn Peak, one of Tuolumne's most recognizable landmarks. The 2.3 mile hike begins at the back side of Tuolumne Meadows Campground (across from the bathrooms for the group camp area), and is just about all uphill. Given the elevation (you climb to about 9,500 feet), it's a good idea to take your time and adopt a slow but steady pace. The water's cold though swimmable, and fishing is fair. Allow from 3 to 4 hours for the 4.6 mile round trip.

❋ **3. Soda Springs.** Here's an easy hike that's flat and perfect for all ages. The trail leads out into the middle of Tuolumne Meadows and a naturally carbonated mineral spring that bubbles mysteriously to the surface. Park in the parking lot just north of the Tioga Road at marker T–32 (just east of the bridge over the Tuolumne River near the campground) adjacent to Lembert Dome. Follow the gravel road to the north, and where the road turns right, walk around the brown metal gate and continue north (if you get to the stables, you're off route). Besides the soda springs, you'll find Parsons Memorial Lodge erected in 1914 by the Sierra Club, and the McCauley Cabin, a pioneer structure now used as a ranger residence. You'll be close to the river and will get a sense of the size and beauty of the meadows. You can make the mile and a half walk in an hour.

❋ **4. Glen Aulin.** To reach this aspen-studded hollow along the Tuolumne River, walk to Soda Springs (see above for trailhead and hiking information). The trail continues past the springs and roughly follows the river 7 miles to a small campground and one of the High Sierra Camps (see page 62). The trail is slightly downhill all the way, and that makes the hike back a stiff one. Watch for Tuolumne Falls and Glen Aulin Falls as you hike. If you are truly a glutton for hiking punishment, Waterwheel Falls, one of the park's most unusual cascades, is 3.3 miles past Glen Aulin. This is a very strenuous hike of 14 miles round trip; give yourself 8 to 10 hours to accomplish it.

❋ **5. Lembert Dome.** From the top of this oddly-shaped dome the 360 degree panorama of Tuolumne Meadows is fantastic. Start at the parking lot at the rock's base which is north of the Tioga Road at marker T–32 (just east of the Tuolumne River). Don't start climbing here; the route is easier and safer up the back of the dome. Follow the nature trail and leave it at marker #2. Climb steeply up the back side of the formation and make your way to the top. Take your topo map for identification of the many peaks and mountains around you. Up and back is about 2.8 miles which should require 3 hours of your time.

❋ **6. Dog Lake.** This easily-reached spot is perfect for swimming and fishing. The hardest part of this 1.5 mile hike is finding the trailhead. At the east end of Tuolumne Meadows turn onto the road which leads to Tuolumne Lodge. Past the Ranger Station and government housing area but before the lodge is a parking lot on the left side of the road. Park there, walk up the embankment to the north, carefully cross the main road, and begin your hike up the hill. The trail is steep at first, then levels off for a final gradual ascent to the lake. A moderate hike of three miles round trip; allow 4 hours.

❋ **7. Lyell Canyon.** If a hike ever fit the definition of a stroll in the park, this is it. The trail will take you to the Lyell Fork of the Tuolumne River and out through the beautiful canyon that shares its name. Begin at the trailhead at the west end of the parking lot for Tuolumne Lodge, but please park your car in the lot described for the Dog Lake hike above. Head into the forest, cross a bridge that seems to want to dump you into the river, then continue to double bridges over the Lyell Fork (less than half a mile out). You can either stay beside the river from this point, or follow the trail which rejoins the river further out the canyon. It's a flat hike the entire route and as scenic and relaxing as they come. Lyell Canyon is about 8 miles long and you can hike as little or as much as you like. Give yourself enough time to make it back before dark.

Camping North of Yosemite Valley

The campgrounds in the north end of the park can be characterized as more primitive and remote and generally smaller (with Tuolumne Meadows Campground being the main exception). Only a few are handled under the Ticketron reservation system, and the balance are operated on a first-come, first-served basis. For campgrounds which can't be reserved in advance, remember that check out time is noon; this is the perfect hour to attempt to obtain a site.

Pets are not allowed in many campgrounds. Check the listings below to see if you can legally bring your pet, and always indicate that you'll be camping with a pet when you make your Ticketron reservation. See page 12 for the specifics of dealing with Ticketron and successfully arranging a campsite reservation.

There are also Ticketron offices at the Big Oak Flat Entrance (where Highway 120 enters the park from the west) and in Tuolumne Meadows (at the entrance to the campground). Oftentimes campsites can be arranged at the last minute by stopping at one of these offices. Call 379-2703 for the Big Oak Flat Ticketron, and 372-4234 for the Tuolumne office.

The summer camping limit is 14 days outside of Yosemite Valley, and most of the campgrounds are open only in summer. The limit extends to 30 days the rest of the year, but you may only camp in Yosemite a total of 30 days in any one calendar year. For general park camping regulations, see page 32.

Hetch Hetchy Area Campgrounds

❋ **Crane Flat Campground:** This camping area of 166 sites is situated at the 6,200 foot level where the Big Oak Flat and Tioga Roads meet. Of all the campgrounds outside of Yosemite Valley, it's the closest—only 17 miles away. The nightly fee is $10, and Ticketron reservations are required. Normally open from May through October, Crane Flat is close to the Merced and Tuolumne Big Tree Groves and the Tioga Road attractions. Pets are allowed.

❋ **Hodgdon Meadow Campground:** Here is the first place to camp when you enter Yosemite from the west on Highway 120 (you'll be 25 miles from Yosemite Valley). All types of campers are welcome in this campground consisting of 105 sites. To reach Hodgdon Meadow, turn down the hill just south of the Big Oak Flat Entrance. It's less than a half mile to the campground entrance. Ticketron reservations are required between May and October ($10 per site); the rest of the year, it's a first-come, first-served facility ($7 per site). Pets are allowed.

Q: Where did Hodgdon Meadow get its name?
A: It's named for Jeremiah Hodgdon, a Vermont native, who homesteaded the area in 1865.

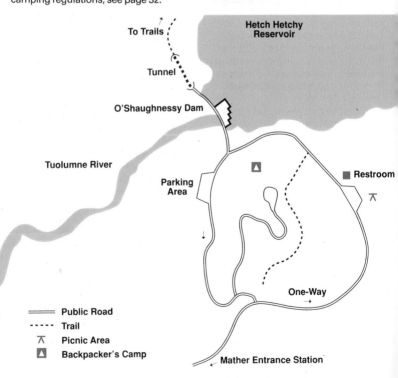

To Trails

Hetch Hetchy Reservoir

Tunnel

O'Shaughnessy Dam

Tuolumne River

Parking Area

■ Restroom

One-Way

Mather Entrance Station

═══ Public Road
----- Trail
🌲 Picnic Area
⛰ Backpacker's Camp

✲ **Hetch Hetchy Backpackers Campground:** Newly constructed, the Hetch Hetchy Campground is exclusively for backpackers and other backcountry users (with wilderness permits) who are beginning their trips from the Hetch Hetchy trailhead. Stays are limited to one night at the beginning and end of backcountry outings. Located at Hetch Hetchy Reservoir, the campground features 19 backpacker sites (6 persons per site), 2 organized group sites (one accommodating 18 persons, the other 25), and 2 stock use sites (6 persons and 6 head of stock per site). Parking is provided near the campground, which has running water and flush toilets. No recreational vehicles, trailers or pets are allowed. Prior arrangements should be made for the organized group and stock use sites. The fees are $2 per night for backpackers and $30 per site for the group and stock sites. Write to the Mather District Office, Star Route, Groveland, CA 95321 or call (209) 372-0323.

Tioga Road Campgrounds

✲ **Tamarack Flat Campground:** If you enjoy a more primitive camping experience (creek water that must be boiled and pit toilets), this campground fits the bill. It's located at 6,300 feet down a three-mile dirt road that takes off the Tioga Road about 6 miles east of Crane Flat (not suitable for large recreational vehicles or trailers). There are 53 campsites, the fee is $4 per night, and it's handled on a first-come, first served basis. Open between June and October. No pets are allowed.

✲ **White Wolf Campground:** A favorite of many high country campers, White Wolf is set on a beautiful meadow alongside a bubbling creek. Added amenities are a stable offering horseback rides, the White Wolf Lodge with a small store and restaurant, and public showers for a fee. The 8,000 foot setting 14 miles east of Crane Flat makes for cold nights and brilliant days. There are 88 first-come, first-served sites which rent for $7. The camping season here is approximately June through October. Pets are allowed.

✲ **Yosemite Creek Campground:** Another primitive campground, the Yosemite Creek camping area is located 5 miles down a narrow dirt road to the south of the Tioga Road (the turnoff is less than a half mile east of the White Wolf junction). Don't, repeat don't, even think about trying to take an RV or a trailer into this campground. The 75 sites utilize pit toilets and water from nearby Yosemite Creek (be sure to treat it). First-come, first-served, $4 per night, and open June through October only. No pets allowed.

✲ **Porcupine Flat Campground:** They call it a flat campground, but there are flatter campgrounds in the world. There's no running water and no flush toilets here, but Porcupine Creek wanders by and the Lodgepole Pines make a fine canopy. Recreational vehicles are limited to a few camp sites at the entry to the area; there are 55 sites total. The fee is $4 per night for these first-come, first-served sites. Open from June through October; no pets are allowed.

✲ **Tenaya Lake Walk-In Campground:** As the name suggests, you must carry your gear on foot into this campground on the western shore of Tenaya Lake. Recreational vehicles, obviously, cannot be accommodated. There are flush toilets, running water and easy access to the lake. This, too, is a first-come, first-served area with 50 sites ($7 per night). Usually open from June through October only. Pets are not allowed.

Tuolumne Meadows Campgrounds

✲ **Tuolumne Meadows Campground:** Here is the park's largest single campground with 330 sites. The road complex throughout the area is complicated and confusing, but once you get the hang of it, you'll love this campground. Families return here year after year for the camping, fishing, hiking and scenery. Ticketron reservations are required for half of the camp sites, the balance are handled on a first-come, first-served basis. There's a store nearby, a restaurant and showers for a fee at Tuolumne Lodge, horseback riding at the stables and fishing in the adjacent Tuolumne River. A sanitary dump station is also available. Backpackers and visitors without vehicles may take advantage of 25 walk-in sites for a fee of $2 per person. Regular sites rent for $10 per night, and the camp is kept open from June through October in a typical year. Pets are allowed.

✲ **Tuolumne Group Campground:** Special camp sites within this campground are available for organized groups by prior arrangement. Reservations must be made at least 12 weeks in advance with Ticketron (see page 14). The fee is $34 per site for now fewer than 10 and no more than 30 people. Parking is provided for up to 5 vehicles per group. No pets are allowed. For more information, call (209) 372-4234.

Gas, Food and Lodging North of Yosemite Valley

Gas

There are two Chevron gas stations in the north portion of Yosemite: one at Crane Flat and the other at Tuolumne Meadows. Given the road closures due to snow, neither is open year round. If you are traveling the Tioga Road, be sure to check your gas gauge as it's a stretch of almost 40 miles where no services are provided. Major credit cards are accepted. Check the *Yosemite Guide* for hours of operation.

A repair garage is open all year in Yosemite Valley, and towing service can be arranged 24 hours a day by calling 372-1221.

Food: Restaurants

The north end of the park is relatively undeveloped. Visitors looking for fine restaurants and *haute cuisine* should try San Francisco or Los Angeles. While there are a few options for hearty meals in generally rustic facilities, you should plan on picnicking a lot and preparing your own food when you travel to Yosemite's north country. The following is a list of your choices (open only during the visitor season of June through October) should you choose to "dine out." Check the *Yosemite Guide* for dates and hours of operation.

✳ **Evergreen Lodge:** Not technically within the park, this old wooden lodge is 7 miles out Evergreen Road on the way to Hetch Hetchy. The simple dining room and unpretentious bar exude an unpolished charm, and at last check, the food was remarkably good. They serve dinner 7 nights a week and breakfast on weekends (lunch items are available at the small store on premises). The Evergreen Lodge is not listed in the *Yosemite Guide*, so call (209) 379-2606 for information on times of operation and to make a reservation. Their normal season is from April through October. Moderate to expensive prices.

✳ **White Wolf Lodge:** With its covered porch and its low-key yet intimate dining room, the White Wolf Lodge, a white-washed wooden structure, is an enjoyable spot to eat. Breakfast and dinner are served from a menu inside (grab a table on the porch if they're serving outdoors), and sandwiches and other items can be purchased from the adjacent store for lunch outside. There's a fine old fireplace, adequate food, and beer and wine. When you consider that the staff gets spread pretty thin with their multiple duties, the service is fine. Dinner reservations are recommended; call 372-1316. Moderate to expensive.

✳ **Tioga Pass Resort:** Here's another spot that fails to qualify as a "park" establishment because it's two miles beyond the Tioga Pass Entrance on Forest Service land. But the place is a Yosemite institution and had to be included. They serve breakfast, lunch and dinner in a room so small that many times you'll be asked to wait for long periods before you can be seated. The wait is worth it, however; try the homemade pies, delicious sandwiches, and substantial breakfasts. Get a load of the classic water spigot with rock-lined drain that's from some other era, and the wonderful curved counter. For reservations, hours, or information, call (209) 372-4471. Moderate prices.

✳ **Tuolumne Meadows Lodge:** The lodge is one of the six High Sierra Camps in Yosemite (see page 62) and the only one accessible by automobile. The dining room is located in a canvas-sided tent-like structure which captures the feeling of roughing it in the high country. But the food will make you think you're someplace fancy. Breakfast and dinner are served from a menu family style; that is, you get seated with whomever happens to be present for mealtime when you are. It's good fun, and many fast friendships have been initiated in the lodge dining room. Beer and wine are served, and box lunches are available upon request. Dinner reservations are required and can be made by calling 372-1313. Moderate to expensive prices.

✳ **Tuolumne Meadows Grill:** Located adjacent to the Tuolumne store and post office, the grill is a great place for a hamburger. The service is as fast as you'll get anywhere, and they pour a big cup of coffee. Pull up a stool or stand and wolf. Fry cooked meals are served at breakfast, lunch and dinner (but the Lodge is preferred for breakfast if you're in no hurry). No reservations accepted (it's not that kind of place), and you can order menu items "to go." Inexpensive prices.

*Inexpensive: dinner for one adult might cost up to $10. Moderate: dinner for one adult might cost from $10 to $20. Expensive: dinner for one adult might cost over $20.

Food: Groceries

The following outlets are basically convenience stores with limited selections. Check the *Yosemite Guide* for operating hours.

✳ **Crane Flat Gas Station:** Located in the main building of the Chevron station at the intersection of the Big Oak Flat and Tioga Roads. Phone 379-2349.

✳ **White Wolf Lodge:** A very small camp store adjacent to the dining room at the lodge. Phone 372-1316.

✳ **Tuolumne Meadows Store:** This facility offers the largest selection and variety north of Yosemite Valley. Phone 372-1328.

Lodging

As in the Wawona area, there are overnight accommodations in the north part of the park which are not operated by the YP&CCo. For reservations for Curry facilities, follow the steps outlined on page 11. You must deal directly with the other independent lodging providers to reserve with them.

The quoted rates for the following listed lodging facilities are approximate only, are based on double occupancy, vary with the seasons, and are subject to change.

✳ **Evergreen Lodge:** Open April through October. Here are 18 rustic cabins on the road to Hetch Hetchy. Nine of them sleep 2 ($50 to $60), the other nine can accommodate up to 4 ($60 to $75). Each cabin includes a private bath, but there are no kitchens. Other amenities are a restaurant, bar and small convenience store. For reservations call directly to (209) 379-2606.

✳ **White Wolf Lodge:** Open in summer only. These rustic accommodations are situated at delightful White Wolf, bordered by meadow and forest both. A few cabins with private bath are available (about $50), along with quite a number of tent cabins that share a communal bathroom and shower house (about $30). Special amenities include a dining room, store, and stable. Reservations should be made through the YP&CCo.

✳ **Tioga Pass Resort:** Open in summer only. Nestled on the side of a hill at well over the 9,000 foot level, the resort consists of 10 housekeeping cabins, 4 motel-type rooms, and a central building with restaurant, store, and gas pumps. It's two miles beyond Tioga Pass Entrance and just outside of the park. Room rates range from $310 to $460 per week, depending on size, and there is no phone. For rate information and reservations write PO Box 7, Lee Vining, CA 93541, or call (209) 372-4471.

✳ **Tuolumne Meadows Lodge:** Open in summer only. Here are 69 canvas tent cabins set close by the Tuolumne River in a picture book setting. The tents are rustic and utilize wood stoves and candles (there's no electricity), but there are mattresses and linen on the beds. Bathrooms and showers are communal and anything but fancy. But that's part of the fun of the Tuolumne Lodge—it's roughing it easy. The tents rent for about $30 and will sleep up to 4. Reservations (which are much sought and highly coveted) should be made through the YP&CCo.

Yosemite's Natural World

Yosemite is filled with living things of every description which exist in a remarkable setting created by the various forces of nature. From its famous black bears and big trees to nocturnal owls, seldom-seen reptiles, pesky mosquitos and mysterious fungi, the park is abundant with flora and fauna that are rich and varied. Because wildlife is protected in Yosemite, it has served as an "island" sanctuary of sorts, where natural processes have continued and biological diversity is still great. Other factors contributing to this favorable situation for animals and plants are the great range of elevations within the park (from 2,000 to 13,000 feet) and the corresponding variety of living conditions which change with the elevation.

Though inanimate, other natural objects and processes contribute to the ever evolving Yosemite scene. Geological workings are constant, waterfalls ebb and flow, and meteorological forces add variety and life to the landscape. And because the setting has been so unchanged and undeveloped, Yosemite National Park is even more significant as a mountain laboratory of the natural world.

Yosemite Geology for Liberal Arts Majors

Most descriptions of Yosemite geology are rife with technical jargon, geological gobbledy gook, and scientific names. This is an attempt to make the processes that created Yosemite's landscape of granite and water more understandable for the layperson. And with it comes the promise that words like batholith, pyroclastic and subduction will not be used.

Once upon a time about 500 million years ago, sediment was deposited in layers on the ocean floor at the west edge of what would later become the continent of North America. This sediment was consolidated into rocks like sandstone, chert, shale and limestone. Neither the land mass of the developing continent nor the land mass covered by sedimentary rock under the ocean was stationary, however.

Time passed (about 300 million years or so) and the two land masses moved towards each other, met, and then some exciting geology took place. The rock beneath the ocean was forced under the continental land mass with interesting results. The process caused the rock of the ocean plate to become very hot and liquefy into magma (which is the molten rock that shoots out of volcanoes). This hot liquid rose up under the edge of the continent to form volcanoes, and where it cooled and hardened before making it to the surface, great areas of granite rock.

This process occurred in a series of pulses over a period of some 150 million years. When it was complete, a mountain range had been formed that ran in a rough line parallel to the west coast. Although it was largely covered by the continental crust (primarily sedimentary rock), this ancestral Sierra Nevada range was probably similar to the present Cascade Range of volcanoes. In some places the mountains may have been as high as 13,000 feet.

For approximately the next 55 million years, the main force at work in the ancestral Sierra was erosion (we all know what that is, right?). The volcanoes were worn away by wind and water as was the continental crust which sat on top of the great granite mass created by the molten rock as described above. The rock that eroded away was carried by rivers and streams into California's Central Valley. When this period of erosion was complete, what was to become the Sierra Nevada, now primarily exposed granite, stood only a few thousand feet high.

Everything was going along fine with the developing Sierra until one day about 25 million years ago, the land masses meeting along the present day San Andreas fault began to move again. The result was that the block upon which the Sierra sat was uplifted at its eastern edge and tilted towards the west. It is estimated that the tilt raised peaks on Yosemite's eastern edge as much as 11,000 feet.

Following uplift and tilt, river courses in the Yosemite region became steeper, and the erosive effect of their waters increased. The Merced River, for example, began to carve the granite much more sharply, and Yosemite Valley was deepened as a canyon. The Sierra Nevada began to show much greater surface relief, and started to take on the form we know today.

About 2 or 3 million years ago, the Earth's climate began to cool. Given its raised height, the Sierra Nevada became covered with glaciers and ice fields along its crest. At its most extensive, the ice covered over half of Yosemite, and sent glaciers down many of the valleys that had been created by the erosion of streams and rivers.

Glaciers tore loose large quantities of rock as they moved, carving u-shaped canyons and valleys, polishing rock faces, and breaking various rock formations like spires and domes along fractures or joints. The glaciers carried the broken rock as rubble and deposited it along the edges of its path.

This glacial period consisted of an unknown number of glaciations — perhaps as many as 10. The last glaciation reached its maximum between 20,000 and 15,000 years ago. At that point, the Earth's climate began to warm again, glaciers receded, and non-glacial erosion became the main geological force working in Yosemite once more.

Yosemite Valley is one location in the park that has changed its appearance considerably since glacial times. Because glaciers dumped enormous quantities of rock and rubble at its western end, the Valley's outflow was stopped and its floor became covered with water. Lake Yosemite was formed. Over the intervening 10,000 years, the lake was filled with sediment, and silt washed down from the park's higher regions, and the Valley's flat, dry floor we know today was created.

Q: What is an erratic boulder?
A: A large rock that has been transported from a distant source by the action of glacial ice. (Look for erratics on Yosemite's peaks and ridges.)

Yosemite's landscape continues to change even now. While the geological processes are not dramatic (some changes take millions of years), erosion continues, avalanches occur, and rockslides are common. The geologic story goes on in Yosemite and provides us with a better understanding of the extraordinary scenery that has made the park famous.

Further Reading

✻ *The Geologic Story of Yosemite National Park* by N. King Huber. Yosemite NP: Yosemite Associaton, 1989.

✻ *Domes, Cliffs & Waterfalls* by William R. Jones. Yosemite NP: Yosemite Association, 1976.

✻ *The Geology of the Sierra Nevada* by Mary Hill. Berkeley: University of California Press, 1975.

✻ *The Incomparable Valley* by Francois E. Matthes. Berkeley: University of California Press, 1950.

Geologists Disagree: Muir vs. Whitney

Nineteenth-century scientists were as puzzled by Yosemite Valley's origin as many first-time visitors are today. Their efforts to explain what they saw resulted in a variety of theories about the creation of the Valley's sheer walls and spectacular waterfalls.

Josiah D. Whitney was the State Geologist for California and Director of the California Geological Survey who made many of the first studies of Yosemite during the 1860's. In his view, Yosemite Valley had not been formed by erosion or glaciation or any other traditional geologic force. He believed that a valley so deep could only have been created by a sudden, catastrophic collapse of that section of the earth below it. Because Whitney was an accomplished Harvard professor with quite a reputation as a scholar and scientist, his theory gained some acceptance.

At about the same time, mountain wanderer John Muir (see page 102) was making observations of his own. He, too, was fascinated with the geologic history of Yosemite Valley. Muir advanced the hypothesis that it was the action of glaciers, an "over-sweeping ice current," that had carved the Yosemite landscape. He worked to popularize the theory and it came to be known as "Muir's discovery."

Whitney was not impressed nor convinced. He characterized Muir's ideas as absurd and passed them off as the ravings of a "mere shepherd." Doggedly, Whitney defended his "cataclysm" theory for some twenty years until his death.

While Muir was not exactly correct in his explanation of the work of the glaciers, he was remarkably close. Later studies proved the basic soundness of this theory and helped establish John Muir's reputation as a thoughtful and insightful student of the Sierra.

Joints Shaped the Rocks

The variety of rock shapes and formations that occur in Yosemite is impressive. From blocks to domes to spires to arches to sheets, there is tremendous diversity in the granitic terrain. How did these structures come to be?

All of Yosemite's unusual landmarks (with but a few exceptions) resulted from the existence of fractures within their original rock structures. These fractures, called joints, are the lines upon which the rocks have been broken. They create zones of weakness within the granite which yield to the action of glaciers and to the intrusion of water.

Joints occur both vertically and horizontally, and some are inclined (for example, the Three Brothers formation was created along inclined joints). Vertical jointing is most prevalent and produced features like the face of Half Dome and the Cathedral Spires. Where vertical and horizontal joints intersect, the result is rectangular blocks.

Half Dome and El Capitan are representative of rocks with very sparse jointing. Their resistance to erosion and glaciation has kept them practically unchanged for thousands of years. Incidentally, there probably is no other half of Half Dome. Geologists believe that only 20% of the dome's original size has been lost.

The type of jointing most dramatic in the evolution of the Yosemite landform is sheeting, the concentric joints that lead to the creation of domes. How these joints form is fairly complicated, but they result mainly from the unloading of the pressure from overlying rock. As relief is experienced, the granite expands upward and fractures result. The concentric fractures break off like the different layers of an onion in a process called exfoliation.

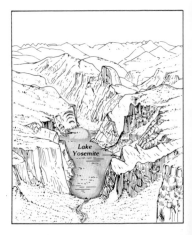

Lake Yosemite

Yosemite Waterfalls

The collection of waterfalls in Yosemite National Park is unequalled anywhere in the world. And nowhere else have so many spectacular waterfalls been concentrated in so small an area as Yosemite Valley. What's most remarkable is the number of park waterfalls that are free-leaping; they make their descent without being broken on intervening ledges or outcroppings. The park's glacial geology is directly responsible for this unique situation.

While the glaciers carved major water courses like Yosemite Valley very deeply, lateral tributary ice streams cut much more slowly and less effectively. The result was "hanging valleys," and streams and creeks which previously had fed directly into primary rivers became routed over the brinks of lofty precipices into the more deeply carved canyons below them. These waters still leap into space over sheer walls as Yosemite's waterfalls today. Good examples of waterfalls originating from hanging valleys are Yosemite Falls and Bridalveil Fall.

Other waterfalls were created as the glaciers moved along and dislocated large blocks of granite from streambeds. The rock gave way along joints (pre-existing fractures where the rock was weak) and took on shapes like steps in a staircase. This was the process responsible for Vernal and Nevada Falls which drop in two major steps from Little Yosemite Valley. Known as the "Giant Staircase," this land form is well-viewed from Glacier Point.

Yosemite's waterfalls are at peak flow during the months of April, May and June when 75% of the annual snow melt occurs. May is usually the best single month for waterfall watching. By July most of the surface runoff is gone, and many falls either dry up or are reduced to a trickle. Some falls rarely dry up because of watersheds with soils that are able to hold more water longer (for example, Bridalveil Fall).

Q: What are ephemeral waterfalls?
A: They are minor waterfalls with small watersheds or falls created by stream flows originating in catch basins that have captured runoff or rainfall. They are characterized by their temporary duration. Examples in Yosemite Valley are Horsetail Fall (on El Capitan) and Staircase Fall below Glacier Point.

BOB JOHNSON 88

Not all the waterfalls in the park are large, spectacular or permanent. Many cascades exist where streambeds were resistant to the glaciers, but some gouging and polishing did occur. In those cases, channels were steepened and now water spills over irregularly fractured granite or down gradual cliff faces. Other falls are ephemeral; they appear only during heavy thunderstorms or at the peak of the spring runoff. As abruptly as the rain ends, so do these fleeting displays.

In winter, park waterfalls have a different beauty. Because the snow pack prevents soil moisture from freezing, water continues to flow in the falls. But they become edged with ice, and droplets of water actually freeze as they descend through space. When this freezing occurs in a large volume, frazil ice is the result. Streams at the base of the waterfalls become filled with ice crystals which create ice slush. As it moves, the frazil ice adheres to any object below freezing, and can clog stream beds.

The most famous winter waterfall phenomenon is the "ice cone" which builds up at the base of Upper Yosemite Fall. As ice slabs which have frozen at the fall's edges fall and gently freezing spray collects, the ice cone grows, sometimes to a height of 300 feet covering some four acres. The cone usually melts away by April.

Further Reading

✳ *Waterfalls of Yosemite Valley* by Michael Osborne. Yosemite NP: Yosemite Association, 1983.

The Legend of Po-ho-no (Bridalveil Fall)

Many snows have come and gone since an old woman and a maiden of Ah-wah-nee were picking berries along the stream above Po-ho-no (Bridalveil Fall). The maiden, looking down the stream to the brink of the fall, was attracted by the mists whirling high into the air. Charmed by the loveliness of the vari-colored cloud she moved down the stream that she might better enjoy the beautiful scene. Gazing into the mists she was drawn, as if hypnotized by some evil spirit, nearer and nearer the brink, until the whirling winds, with a shriek of unholy glee, whipped her up and carried her over the fall to her death on the rocks below.

The old woman, terrified by what she had seen, quickly made her way down the cliff, and into the camp, crying that Po-ho-no, "The Spirit of the Evil Wind," had drawn the maiden into his clutches. The old chief of Ah-wah-nee then warned all in his tribe never to venture within the spray or mists of Po-ho-no, as it was the abode of an evil spirit who would draw them to their death, and carry their spirit down into his land of darkness and misery, there to hold it captive until he secured another.

So solemnly was this warning given that to this day no one has ever known a son or daughter of Ah-wah-nee to venture into the spray or mists of Po-ho-no.
— from *Legends of the Yosemite Miwok* compiled by Frank LaPena & Craig D. Bates (Yosemite Association, 1981).

The Ten Highest Waterfalls in the World

1.	Angel Fall	3,212 ft.	free falling	Venezuela
2.	Tugela Falls	3,110 ft.	series of falls	South Africa
3.	**Yosemite Falls**	2,425 ft.	series of falls	Yosemite
4.	**Sentinel Falls**	2,000 ft.	series of falls	Yosemite
5.	**Snow Creek Falls**	2,000 ft.	series of falls	Yosemite
6.	Cuquenan Fall	2,000 ft.	free falling	Venezuela
7.	Sutherland Falls	1,904 ft.	series of falls	New Zealand
8.	Mardalsfoss Falls	1,696 ft.	series of falls	Norway
9.	Takakkaw Falls	1,650 ft.	series of falls	Canada
10.	**Ribbon Fall**	1,612 ft.	free falling	Yosemite

Waterfalls of Yosemite Valley

Yosemite Falls	2,425 ft.	North wall, eastern end
Sentinel Falls	2,000 ft.	South wall, west of Sentinel Rock
Ribbon Fall	1,612 ft.	North wall, west of El Capitan
Staircase Falls	1,300 ft.	South wall, behind Curry Village
Royal Arch Cascade	1,250 ft.	North wall, west of Washington Column
Silver Strand Falls	1,170 ft.	South wall, far west end
El Capitan Falls	1,000 ft.	North wall, east side of El Capitan
Lehamite Falls	uncertain	North wall, in Indian Canyon
Bridalveil Fall	620 ft.	South wall, west end
The Cascades	uncertain	North wall, 2 miles west of Yosemite Valley
Nevada Fall	594 ft.	Easternmost end of Merced River Canyon
Illilouette Fall	370 ft.	Panorama Cliffs southeast of Glacier Point
Vernal Fall	317 ft.	East of Happy Isles on Merced River

Yosemite Plantlife

There are over 1,500 different types of plants in Yosemite. They range from the grand sequoias to tiny fungi and lichen. What follows is a brief overview of Yosemite flora with information on how to find out much more.

Trees

Both cone-bearing and broad-leaved trees appear in abundance within Yosemite National Park. The trees that bear cones (also known as conifers) do not shed all of their leaves or needles on an annual basis which has led to their designation as "evergreens." The broad-leaved trees drop their leaves each year.

✻ **The Conifers:** There are at least 18 different species of conifers that occur in the park. About half of them are pines. Most common at lower elevations are the Ponderosa (or Yellow) Pine and the Jeffrey Pine. The Ponderosa is abundant in Yosemite Valley, has yellow-orange bark, needles in groups of three, bark scales that fit together like a jigsaw puzzle, and a trunk up to six feet in diameter. The Jeffrey Pine looks much like the Ponderosa but grows at higher elevations (Glacier Point is a typical locality). If in doubt, smell the bark. The Jeffrey exudes a sweet odor like vanilla or pineapple.

The two typical high-elevation pines are the Lodgepole and the White Bark. The Lodgepole has needles in twos, yellowish bark and small cones. The White Bark features needles in bunches of five, purplish, pitchy cones, and tends to be dwarfed at timber line.

Other notable conifers are the red and white firs. Large forests of these trees can be seen along the Tioga and Glacier Point Roads. White firs occur between 3,500 and 8,000 feet and have 2-inch needles that twist off the branch and 3 to 5 inch cones. Red firs, in contrast, have shorter needles that curl upwards and larger cones (5 to 8 inches), and grow between 6,000 and 9,000 feet.

Q: What species are the large pine trees that sport long cones hanging from their upper branches like Christmas tree ornaments?

A: Sugar pine. Because the trees yield great quantities of even-grained, clear wood that is excellent for building, most of the forests of sugar pine in California were harvested during the 19th century.

✳ **Broad-Leaved Trees:** Almost without exception, these trees lose their leaves in the fall (they are deciduous). As the leaves die as part of this annual process, they take on different hues such as orange, yellow and brown. It is the foliage of the broad-leaved trees, then, that provides us with sometimes spectacular "fall color." These deciduous trees are less varied than the conifers.

There are many types of oaks in the park. In Yosemite Valley the California Black Oak is distinctive. It grows to heights of 75 feet, has dark grey to black bark, and produces large acorns that the Yosemite Indians used as a staple in their diet. The other common oak is the Canyon Live Oak, which has holly-like evergreen leaves.

Other conspicuous broad-leaved trees are the Pacific Dogwood which produces beautiful and delicate whitish-green flowers each spring, and the Quaking Aspen known for its paper-thin white bark and the rustling of its often-colorful leaves with the slightest breeze.

Along streams and rivers, particularly at lower elevations, one will encounter cottonwoods (leaves are bright green on top and light below), willows (slender pointed leaves) and alders (dark green leaves with obvious veins and small teeth).

Flowering Plants

The spectacular geography of Yosemite with its elevations ranging from 2,000 to over 13,000 feet, supports a natural wildflower garden without equal, not to mention shrubs, grasses, ferns and fungi. The differing temperatures, precipitation levels and growing seasons insure that many assorted plants find conditions to their liking at locations throughout the park.

The blooming season is a long one in Yosemite. It starts in the foothills in April and May and gradually moves upslope as the weather warms and the snow melts. It doesn't reach the park's highest elevations until August when flowers appear for a brief two month appearance. All told, the wildflower season in Yosemite lasts a full six months!

For the student of botany, Yosemite is indeed a remarkable classroom. Within the park is some of the most distinctive and unique vegetation in the world. Because natural processes have been allowed to continue and because little disruption of the physical environment has occurred, plantlife is varied and rich.

Taking the time to learn about Yosemite's wildflowers (and other plants) can be amazingly rewarding. Being able to identify the various flowers and plants you encounter will enrich your park experience.

Further Reading

✳ *Discovering Sierra Trees* by Stephen F. Arno. Yosemite NP: Yosemite Association and Sequoia Natural History Association, 1973.

✳ *Pacific Coast Tree Finder* by Tom Watts. Berkeley: Nature Study Guild, 1973.

✳ *Yosemite Wildflower Trails* by Dana Morgenson. Yosemite NP: Yosemite Association, 1975.

✳ *Wildflowers of Yosemite* by Lynn and Jim Wilson and Jeff Nicholas. Yosemite NP: Sunrise Productions, 1987.

✳ *A Sierra Nevada Flora* by Norman F. Weeden. Berkeley: Wilderness Press, 1975.

Q: What is the strange red plant (with no leaves or green of any kind) that is noticeable on the forest floor each spring?

A: Snow plant (Sarcoides sanguinea). A "saprophyte," it lives on decayed organic matter, appearing just after the snow melts each year.

The Giant Sequoias

A mature sequoia tree is 3,125,000,000, 000,000,000,000 times larger than a single bacterium.
— J.I.D. Hinds

After its granite cliffs and domes and its spectacular waterfalls, Yosemite is best known for its famous big trees, the giant sequoias. In fact, the 1864 Yosemite Grant set aside as a protected park only Yosemite Valley and the Mariposa Grove of Big Trees. These towering monarchs were recognized for their special qualities early in history, and they continue to inspire awe to this day.

The mature big trees can be recognized by their huge, columnar trunks which are free of branches for 100 to 150 feet. The foliage is blue-green and individual leaves create rounded sprays, unlike the flattened branchlets of the incense cedar. The bark is quite fibrous, can be 4 to 24 inches thick, and is cinnamon brown in color. This bark covering is non-resinous and very fire-resistant. Sequoia wood is pink when cut, then darkens to red. It is amazingly resistant to decay (many downed trees remain intact on the ground for years). Cones are quite small (2 or 3 inches), are abundant, and produce several hundred seeds each.

The giant sequoias *(Sequoiadendron giganteum)* grow from these tiny seeds which are no larger than flakes of oatmeal. You would have to amass over 90,000 seeds to produce a pound of them. Upon germination, a one inch seedling results, and these seedlings grow into young trees through the years. These youngsters are characterized by a fairly symmetrical, cone-shaped appearance with sharply-pointed crowns.

Middle age is reached by sequoias when they are 700 or 800 years old. They are mature, have just about reached their maximum height, and have developed a rounded top. Some mature trees that have been burned are noted for their "snag tops." When fire damages the bases of the trees, water supply to the tops is limited and the tops of the trees die. The trees remain healthy, but their appearance suggests the hazards and effects of age.

Scientists believe that the giant sequoia is the largest living thing in the world (though this is sometimes disputed). The trees stop growing upward at about 800 years of age, but they continue to add bulk. Maximum height seems to be about 320 feet, and diameters at the base vary depending on where the measurements are taken (there is quite a swelling at the base of each sequoia). Some trees at the base are over 35 feet in diameter, while at about 20 feet above the ground, that size drops to about 20 feet.

It is hard to grasp the enormity of the sequoias. One example that provides perspective is the largest branch on the Grizzly Giant tree in the Mariposa Grove. It is over 6 feet in diameter. At that size it is larger than the trunks of the largest specimens of most trees east of the Mississippi River. It is also larger than many of the conifers in Yosemite.

Despite their longevity, giant sequoias are not the oldest living things. That distinction is reserved for the bristlecone pines which may live to be 5,000 years old. Sequoias are known to live at least 3,200 years, and John Muir reported finding an individual 4,000 years old.

Giant sequoias occur naturally only in the Sierra Nevada primarily at elevations between 5,000 and 7,000 feet. In Yosemite there are three big tree groves: the Mariposa Grove (see page 46), the Tuolumne Grove, and the Merced Grove (page 56). Any visit to Yosemite should include a trip to see these impressive trees.

Further Reading

✳ *The Sequoias of Yosemite National Park* by H. Thomas Harvey. Yosemite NP: Yosemite Association, 1978.

✳ *Giant Sequoias* by H.T. Harvey, H.S. Shellhammer, R.E. Stecker and R.J. Hartesveldt. Three Rivers, CA: Sequoia Natural History Association, 1981.

✳ *The Enduring Giants* by Joseph H. Engbeck, Jr. Sacramento: California Dept. of Parks and Recreation, 1973.

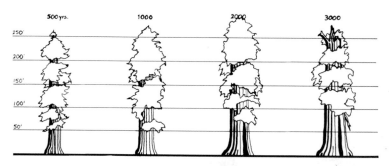

Mammals

Over 75 species of mammals have been recorded in Yosemite National Park. What follows is a brief description of some of those mammals, particularly those that are likely to be seen by visitors in the course of their stay in the park.

Mule Deer

Having experienced a life free of threat from humans, the mule deer in Yosemite seem almost tame. You are likely to spot one or more of these graceful creatures anywhere in the park, but they are particularly obvious in Yosemite Valley and in the Wawona meadow area.

Despite the fact that they seem unconcerned by humans, mule deer should be treated as any other wild animal. These deer should be given a wide berth and not be fed (nor should any other park animal); many injuries have been caused to visitors who have disturbed these animals in the course of offering them human food. Even deaths have resulted from gorings and from the blows delivered by the surprisingly sharp hooves of the mule deer. In fact, more injuries occur in Yosemite inflicted by deer each year than those caused by black bears or any other park animal.

The mule deer takes its name from its large, mule-like ears. Weighing up to 200 pounds, it is primarily a browse animal eating leaves and tender twigs from trees, grass and other herbs. The male mule deer (the buck) grows antlers each year for use in the mating season or "rut" each fall. Despite popular belief, the age of a given buck cannot be determined by counting the number of antler points he sports.

Mule deer are very common in Yosemite and are seen chiefly between 3,500 and 8,500 feet. They stay below the snow line in winter, often dropping into the foothills that border the west side of the park. Common predators of the mule deer are the mountain lion and the coyote.

Black Bear

The reaction of many people to the black bear is both fascination and fear. Because of the many stories that are told about bears throughout the national park system, there are plenty of misconceptions that exist about these largest of park mammals.

Yosemite's black bear is often confused with the grizzly bear, a species that no longer exists in the park. The grizzly once roamed the Sierra Nevada but was eliminated by hunters around the turn of the century. The last grizzly killing occurred in Yosemite in 1895, and the last authentic record of the killing of a grizzly in California was 1922.

Grizzly bears are considerably more dangerous to humans than are black bears. Occasional incidents do occur, but those mainly result from improper food storage by visitors. For information about storing your food properly, see pages 17 & 32. Never feed the bears, and observe them at a distance (particularly when cubs are present)!

Despite their name, black bears can be brown, blonde, cinnamon or black. There are no members of the brown bear species (or any other) in Yosemite. Individuals range in size from 250 to 500 pounds, although even bigger bears have been recorded.

These bears are omnivores — they will eat practically anything. Typical fare is insects, small rodents, berries, acorns and seeds. But human food, from hot dogs to cookies, also appeals to park bears. Because dependence on a human-provided diet creates bears which become bold and are not afraid of people, the need to keep visitor food well-stored is even more acute.

Black bears can be observed throughout the park, particularly in the evenings. Many bears enter a den in winter for a period of sleep that is not true hibernation. Young are born in late winter and leave the den in spring to forage with their mother.

Tricks for Observing Park Animals

Try strolling down a forest trail, or walk along the edge of a meadow. Avoid groups of people, as most animals are easily frightened. Consider the color of your clothing and don't wear white, it makes you too conspicuous. Darker shades are better. Walk slowly. When you see an animal, don't make quick movements. If you should come upon one, such as a deer or a squirrel, continue slowly so as not to alarm it. Stop to watch it when you are still some distance away. If you want to see an animal that has disappeared into a burrow — a marmot, ground squirrel or a mouse — find a comfortable place to sit and remain quiet. Usually it will reappear in a short time to see where you are and what you are doing. Watch for evidences of mammal activities, such as dens, trails in the grass, or piles of kitchen middens where squirrels have cut away the scales of pine cones. Watch, too, for holes dug where pine nuts or acorns have been buried.
— from *Discovering Sierra Mammals*

Coyote

Normally a very shy mammal, the Yosemite coyote has become accustomed to the human presence and is commonly seen here, particularly in Yosemite Valley. In winter, these dog-like creatures can often be viewed hunting in snow-covered meadows.

The coyote is one mammal that makes its presence known by its call. There is nothing more haunting (some would contend frightening) than the late-night howling and barking of a group of coyotes.

Weighing 25 to 30 pounds, coyotes live on small animals (primarily rodents) although fawns and an occasional adult mule deer are taken. They can be identified by their long, grayish fur (which is lighter on the underside) and a darkish tail.

Squirrels and Chipmunks

A variety of squirrels and chipmunks is present in Yosemite. Most visitors, particularly campers, will encounter one or more species of these active rodents.

The common squirrels are the California Gray Squirrel (all gray with a long bushy tail, often seen in trees), the Sierra Chickaree (a reddish tree squirrel that chews on pine cones and squeaks alot), and the California Ground Squirrel (a brown animal, speckled with white, which lives in burrows in the ground). At higher elevations, the common ground squirrel is the "Picket Pin" (or Belding ground squirrel) which seated in its erect posture looks like a stake driven into the ground.

There are at least 5 different chipmunks in the park. They are generally reddish brown in color, smaller than the squirrels, and wear 4 light-colored stripes separated by dark on their backs. These chipmunks are remarkably animated and quick, and dig burrows in stumps or the ground which are very hard to find.

MARMOT

Marmot

A common sight in the park's higher elevations is the yellow-bellied marmot; watch for these rotund fellows at Olmsted Point on the Tioga Road. Actually members of the squirrel family, marmots resemble woodchucks for which they are sometimes mistaken. They regularly sun themselves on subalpine rocks, and behave tamely at certain roadside turnouts. Please do not feed them.

The marmots are about 15 to 18 inches long and have an average weight of about 5 pounds. They are yellowish-brown, live in dens under rock piles or tree roots, and hibernate during the winter. Their shrill warning note is distinctive.

Big Horn Sheep

Originally native to the Yosemite area, the California bighorn sheep were eliminated here around 1900 as a result of hunting and the disease spread by domestic animals.

In 1986, a herd of bighorns was released in the Tioga Pass area of Yosemite in an effort by scientists and researchers to re-establish a viable population. To date the experiment has been a success. Additional transplants have augmented the herd which has been able to reproduce and survive on its own.

Bighorn sheep are remarkable rock climbers able to ascend and descend amazingly steep terrain. Some sheep weigh up to 200 pounds and are 3 feet high at the shoulder. They are gray or buffy brown in color and grow hard, permanent horns. In the male, they spriral back sometimes into a full circle, while the females have small, slightly backward curving horns. Watch for these beautiful animals in the mountainous regions around Tioga Pass.

Other Mammals

These brief descriptions have touched on but a few of the numerous mammals native to Yosemite. To learn more, consult the following books which will provide greater depth and detail.

Further Reading

✻ *Discovering Sierra Mammals* by Russell K. Grater. Yosemite NP: Yosemite Association and Sequoia Natural History Association, 1978.

✻ *Sierra Nevada Natural History* by Tracy I. Storer and Robert L. Usinger. Berkeley: University of California Press, 1963.

Birds

Because Yosemite plays host to over 240 different kinds of birds, it is not practical to provide an exhaustive and detailed bird list here. As was the case with the mammals, the following are highlights of the species one is likely to encounter in the course of a visit.

Steller's Jay

This is, undoubtedly, one bird that just about everybody notices in Yosemite. The jay is bright blue with a dark head and a very prominent crest. Unfazed by humans, it boldly alights on tables and other perches close to food, all the while screeching its disagreeable screech. Surprisingly, the Steller's jay also is capable of producing a soft, warbling song. When a group of jays encounters a hawk or owl, the raucous cacophony of shrieks and calls that results is almost overpowering.

Acorn Woodpecker

In Yosemite Valley, the acorn woodpecker is the woodpecker you are likely to see. Black and white with a red head marking (sometimes there's yellow also), these industrious birds drill holes in trees, telephone poles and buildings and fill them with acorns that they eat later. Their flight is a distinctive series of shallowly u-shaped glides, and they are exceptionally noisy, making a "wack-up, wack-up" call most often. Wherever you find oaks, you will find acorn woodpeckers.

Western Tanager

Here is a bird that is hard to miss. Though not common, the tanager is bright yellow with a bright orangish-red head. Likely to be seen in Yosemite Valley in spring and summer, this gaudy bird will sometimes come to your picnic table or the ground near you. This may be the only bird in Yosemite with "day-glo" feathers.

Belted Kingfisher

Along the Merced River and other bodies of water in the park, this striking blue bird can be seen flying low or perched on branches and snags, watching for fish and aquatic insects. If you're lucky, one will plunge into the water and emerge with dinner in its beak. There is a noticeable crest and a reddish band on the chest. You'll know it's a kingfisher if you hear a loud rattling, clicking call.

American Dipper

Another water bird, the dipper is truly phenomenal. Though gray and nondescript, these acrobatic creatures are named for their habit of bobbing up and down almost constantly. What's so phenomenal about them is their ability to fly into a stream or river and walk upstream underwater along the bottom clinging to rocks as they search for food. As you stroll beside a stream or river, keep a close eye for the amazing dipper!

Clark's Nutcracker

The high country counterpart of the Steller's Jay is the Clark's Nutcracker. Also known as the "camp robber," this white, gray and black bird with a prominent beak has a harsh, cawing voice. Very conspicuous in areas around Tuolumne Meadows, the Clark's Nutcracker does crack and eat pine nuts, but is not averse to cleaning up around your campsite. You'll see these birds typically above 9,000 feet.

AMERICAN DIPPER

Black-headed Grosbeak

While picnicking or camping, you may see this other common Yosemite Valley resident. The grosbeak is characterized by its black, white and orange markings and by its "gross beak" which is used for opening seeds. Oftentimes the woods echo with the grosbeak's delightfully lyrical song which has been called a rich warble. The black-headed grosbeak is a sure sign of spring.

Great Horned Owl

You may never get a glimpse of this bird, but chances are good you may hear one. This nocturnal dweller of most of the park's life zones is active from dusk until dawn. Most of that time it issues a series of deep, sonorous hoots. If you happen to hear the horned one, see if you can locate its perch. These owls are excellent ventriloquists, so don't be surprised if you fail. Large ear tufts are sure signs that you've found the great horned owl.

Other Birds

There's a whole lot to be learned about Yosemite's birds, and plenty of ways to learn it. Try a ranger-led bird walk, or pick up a pair of binoculars and see what there is to see. The books listed are great guides and will make your bird education easier for you.

Yosemite's Ten "Most Wanted" Birds

Serious, sometimes fanatic, birdwatchers (or "birders") often keep a list of every bird known to occur in North America; it's known as their personal "life list." When they see a bird they've never seen before, they will check it off the list. The goal is to see every single species on the list. There are several birds in Yosemite which are rarely seen anywhere else. These "most wanted" birds are feverishly sought by many zealous birdwatchers for their life lists.

1. Great Gray Owl
2. Peregrine Falcon
3. Rosy Finch
4. Black-Backed Three-Toed Woodpecker
5. Flammulated Owl
6. Northern Goshawk
7. Pileated Woodpecker
8. Williamson's Sapsucker
9. Northern Pygmy Owl
10. Black Swift

Further Reading

✳ *Discovering Sierra Birds* by Ted Beedy and Steve Granholm. Yosemite NP: Yosemite Association and Sequoia Natural History Association, 1985.

✳ *Birds of Yosemite and the East Slope* by David Gaines. Lee Vining, Ca.: Artemisia Press, 1988.

GOSHAWK, BY STEVE HICKMAN

Reptiles and Amphibians

Lizards, frogs and snakes are all members of this group of Yosemite wildlife. About 40 different species of amphibians and reptiles are known to have established populations in the Yosemite Sierra, and there are no doubt more.

All of the lizards in Yosemite are harmless reptiles. Because they prefer warm locations, they are found primarily in the lower elevations of the park (Yosemite Valley and below). Most commonly seen is the Western Fence Lizard. He's black or blotched brownish-gray on top with a blue throat and belly.

At least 14 different types of snakes inhabit the park. With the exception of the Western Rattlesnake, they are all non-poisonous. The most regularly seen species is the garter snake which frequents meadows, ponds, streams and lakes (it's a remarkably good swimmer). The garter snake is black, gray or dark brown with a cream colored strip down its back and usually red blotches on its sides.

The Western rattlesnake is Yosemite's only venomous snake, but rarely bites people. The rattler varies from cream to black in color with a variety of blotches. The head is broad, flat and triangular, and when surprised, the snake will coil and shake the rattles it sports at the end of its tail. The result is a buzzing sound which is a warning to stay away.

Frogs and toads are abundant in Yosemite; there are a minimum of 8 different kinds. You are more likely to hear from these denizens of the park than to see them. Most abundant is the Pacific treefrog, a small, green, gray or brown fellow with a black mask and a constantly heard year-round song. Recently it has been determined that the Mountain Yellow-Legged frog, quite common 20 and 30 years ago, is in steep decline and possibly disappearing from the park.

The last of the amphibians are the salamanders and newts. These small, slimy creatures like it moist and dark. That's why they're rarely seen. Most likely to be discovered is the California newt, the brownish-orange newt that is often spotted after a heavy rain. Two species of salamander are found almost nowhere else but in the Yosemite region: the Mt. Lyell and the Limestone salamanders.

Further Reading

⁜ *Discovering Sierra Reptiles and Amphibians* by Harold Basey. Yosemite NP: Yosemite Association and Sequoia Natural History Association, 1976.

⁜ *California Amphibians and Reptiles* by Robert C. Stebbins. Berkeley: University of California Press, 1972.

Q: Can rattlesnakes swim?

A: Yes, quite well. Their long right lungs provide increased buoyancy. They usually hold their rattles high and dry and may strike while in water.

Fishes

Despite the impression of many people that the Yosemite region is dotted with lakes and streams laden with native trout, there is only one game fish that naturally occurs in the park. That's the rainbow trout. There are five other native species, but they are relatively uncommon and are not game fishes (the Sacramento sucker, the Sacramento squawfish, the hardhead, the California roach, and the riffle sculpin).

When the glaciers moved through Yosemite during the last ice age, native fish populations were eliminated and most of the park's lakes and streams were left fish-less. When the U.S. Army managed Yosemite National Park between 1890 and 1914, one job it undertook was to plant new fish species in the high country and provide greater opportunities for sport fisherpeople. Non-native species that were introduced and now occur in the park are the cutthroat trout, the golden trout, the brown trout, and the brook trout. The brook and brown trouts have adapted best.

For information about fishing in Yosemite, see page 27. For additional, more in-depth coverage of the park's fish family, see the sources at right.

A List of the Fishes of Yosemite National Park ("N" denotes a native species)

✳ Trout
Brook Trout *(Salvelinus fontinalis)*
Brown Trout *(Salmo trutta)*
Cutthroat Trout *(Salmo clarkii)*
Golden Trout *(Salmo aguabonita)*
Rainbow Trout *(Salmo gairdnerii)* N

✳ Suckers
Sacramento Sucker *(Catostomus occidentalis)* N

✳ Minnows
California Roach *(Hesperoleucus symmetricus)* N
Hardhead *(Mylopharodon conocephalus)* N
Sacramento Squawfish (Ptychocheilus grandis) N

✳ Sculpins
Riffle Sculpin *(Cottus gulosus)* N

Further Reading

✳ *Fishes of Yosemite National Park* by Willis A. Evans, Orthello Wallis and Glenn D. Gallison. Yosemite NP: Yosemite Natural History Association, 1961. (Presently out of print).

✳ *Yosemite Trout Fishing* by Hank Johnston. Yosemite NP: Flying Spur Press, 1985.

✳ *Sierra Trout Guide* by Ralph Cutter. Portland: Frank Amato Publications, 1984.

Q: What is the oldest record of trout planting in Yosemite Valley?
A: April 1, 1879, when the Yosemite Fish Commission began planting 20,000 young trout in the different streams of the Valley.

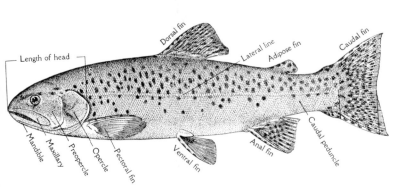

The Poisonous, The Itchy and The Sickening

The relatively undeveloped landscape of Yosemite Valley and the vast regions of wilderness around it are home to plants, animals and other organisms that may in one way or another be hazardous to your health. The threat from these sources is generally not serious, and there are a number of precautions you can take and signs to watch for to avoid problems. Whatever you do, don't become frightened by the following list.

Rattlesnakes

These wriggly reptiles are the only poisonous snakes in Yosemite. Out hiking, you will rarely encounter a rattler, and if you do it will almost always buzz its rattles when threatened. If you happen upon a rattlesnake, keep a safe distance and leave. Do not try to kill it or scare it away. It's always a good idea to watch carefully where you walk, where you put your hands and where you sit.

Scorpions

In Yosemite's lower elevations, this threatening-looking insect hides by day and becomes active at night. The sting delivered by the scorpion is painful but not at all dangerous to humans. Scorpions hide under rocks and logs, so be cautious when you're lifting and rolling such objects.

Giardia Lamblia

This funny sounding creature is a protozoan which causes an intestinal disease called giardiasis. Its symptoms are chronic diarrhea, abdominal cramps, bloating, fatigue and weight loss. Because giardia has been found to be present in park lakes and streams, you should purify any drinking water that is not from the tap. Either boil it for at least a minute, use an iodine-based purifier, or use   giardia-rated water filter.

Mosquitos

These delightful insects have been characterized by one writer as the "most bothersome of the animal life in the High Sierra." Though relatively benign individually, roving bands of mosquitos can make the lives of visitors, particularly in certain areas of the backcountry, totally miserable. They breed in locations with standing water, so they are common wherever there is snow melt. Typically, that means 4,000 feet at the end of May advancing upwards to 10,000 feet by late July. What can be done about these pesky pests? Try repellents, long pants and long-sleeved shirts, and mosquito-net hats and tents. If you're backpacking, locate your camp to take advantge of any breeze and away from areas of moisture.

Ticks

Some park ticks, the small insects that suck blood from a variety of mammals, carry an illness known as Lyme disease. Not every tick, however, is a carrier. Symptoms of the disease in its advanced form can include arthritis, meningitis, neurological problems and cardiac symptoms, and the disease can be very serious. If it is detected early, treatment can cure or lessen the severity of the disease. If you think you might have been bitten by a tick, watch for a rash at the spot of the bite and for symptoms of the flu. If you contract Lyme disease and you believe its source was Yosemite, please call the Park Sanitarian at (209) 372-0288.

Poison Oak

This is one of the most widespread shrubs in California which is abundant in Yosemite's lower reaches. Fluids from the plant produce an irritating rash on the skin of humans which can sometimes be very severe. Sufferers itch terrifically and can experience swelling. If you think you've been in poison oak, wash your body and clothes thoroughly to remove the oily fluid.

Spiders

There are a couple of interesting critters in this category. The single truly dangerous spider in Yosemite is the black widow. With its black, orb-shaped body featuring a red "hour glass" pattern on its underside, this arachnid is easy to identify. The black widow is not aggressive, but when disturbed can bite and inject a nerve poison which can cause severe symptoms and even death. If bitten, see a physician quickly. Much more fearsome in appearance is the tarantula, but this big, woolly fellow is fairly benign. Up to four inches across, tarantulas are active at night and don't bite unless provoked. The bite is painful but not dangerous.

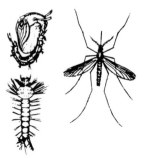

Yosemite's Endangered Species

While Yosemite National Park is abundant with varied plant and animal life, indigenous species have been lost to extinction over the years, and threats to park life forms persist despite the National Park Service's best efforts to protect them. Grizzly bears were once residents of the Yosemite Sierra, and other birds, mammals and plants have been lost.

But the picture is not entirely dreary. New resource and research programs implemented in recent years have resulted in major strides in species protection and enhancement. A good example is the 1986 reintroduction of the Sierra Nevada bighorn sheep to the Tioga Pass area.

Because of extensive hunting and the devastating effects of diseases communicated by domestic sheep, the bighorns disappeared from the Yosemite region in the 1890s. Many feared these hoofed mountaineers would never again be seen atop park pinnacles. But through an inter-agency effort involving both State and Federal bureaus, and with funding from private sources, 27 bighorn sheep were transplanted from a herd in the Southern Sierra to Lee Vining Canyon. Since that original reintroduction, supplemental transplants have been made, and the herd appears to be reproducing successfully and actually increasing in population.

Not all threats to park wildlife are controllable at Yosemite. Take the Peregrine falcon. These impressive flyers eat birds that migrate to Central and South America each winter. Use of pesticides is much more common in these wintering areas, and DDT has found its way into the systems of many Yosemite Peregrines. The result is that the eggs they lay are thin-shelled and subject to breakage. Nesting success dropped dramatically, and park officials feared that Peregrines might be lost for good.

But through a fairly complicated augmentation procedure, the National Park Service is seeing a growth in Peregrine numbers and nests. During the nesting season, climbers are employed to reach Peregrine nests and remove the fragile eggs. They are replaced with plastic phonies. Captive-raised chicks are later placed in the nests, and the parents adopt the newcomers without hesitation. In the meantime, work is being done to encourage other countries to limit their use of harmful chemicals.

Other significant programs have involved the restoration of meadows, oak woodlands and other park areas.

As well, a number of revegetation efforts are underway to reclaim portions of Yosemite that have been overused and stripped of any plantlife. Watch for evidence of this important work as you travel throughout the park, and be sure your use of Yosemite is consistent with the protection of the plants and animals here.

It's encouraging to know that strides such as these have been made, but NPS employees remain constantly on the alert for new threats to Yosemite's natural world. The future health of the park depends on their success with this critical task.

Yosemite Species Listed As At Risk by the US Government

Endangered

* Peregrine Falcon
* Southern Bald Eagle
* Yosemite Woolly Sunflower

Threatened

* Congdon's Lewisia
* Congdon's Woolly Sunflower

Yosemite Species Listed As At Risk by the State of California

Endangered

* Congdon's Lewisia
* Congdon's Woolly Sunflower
* Great Gray Owl
* Peregrine Falcon
* Southern Bald Eagle
* Thompson's Sedge
* Yosemite Onion

Rare

* Sierra Nevada Bighorn Sheep
* Sierra Nevada Red Fox
* Wolverine

Yosemite History

The recorded history of Yosemite National Park is as fascinating and important as it is short relative to that of other parts of our country and the world. While Native Americans were long-term residents, Yosemite Valley was not entered by whites until 1851, and not really occupied by them in any meaningful way until the last quarter of the nineteenth century.

These historical events are particularly significant because the actions of both men and governments in and relating to Yosemite proved to be pioneering efforts in the conservation of natural areas all around the globe. There is little question that at Yosemite the concept of National Parks was born, and the park still serves as a model and symbol for the entire world.

Yosemite's Native People

Indians resided in the Yosemite region for about 4,000 years before the Spaniards occupied California and the Gold Rush occurred. Anthropologists suggest that the earliest Indian inhabitants came from the East side of the Sierra Nevada looking for water and food in particularly dry years. Later, groups from the Central Valley (predominantly Miwok-speaking) invaded the foothills and greater Yosemite as Indian populations increased and competition for homeland grew. The Miwoks and the people from the east side came together and established permanent villages near the Merced River throughout Yosemite Valley.

Obviously, there is no recorded history of the Yosemite Miwoks until very recent times. Anthropologists believe that the Miwok culture evolved very slowly. Their simple lifestyle remained relatively unchanged, no doubt, for centuries. The Yosemites' basically primitive existence involved seed and plant gathering, hunting and trading. Generally, they spent fall and winter in Yosemite Valley or the warmer foothills, then roamed into Yosemite's high country in spring and summer in quest of game and to barter with Mono Lake Paiutes and other people from east of the area.

Indian people in California were brought in contact with whites with the advent of the Spanish missions in the late 18th century. As the central and southern parts of the state became settled, white encroachment on traditional Indian territory increased. There is no evidence of this fact, but some believe that at the beginning of the 1800's the Indian people of Yosemite were struck with a "fatal black sickness," a plague of some type. Reportedly, the few survivors abandoned the Valley and relocated to the Eastern Sierra and were assimilated by other groups there. For a number of years (the exact number unknown), Yosemite Valley may have been uninhabited.

One of the offspring of the Yosemite people who grew up with the Mono Paiutes was Tenaya (see page 101). As a youth, Tenaya had heard stories of the beauty and bounty of Yosemite Valley. He finally visited the former home of his people quite late in his life. Being favorably impressed, he and 200 other Indians (some Yosemite Miwoks, some not) resettled the Valley. Tenaya was named Chief of the group.

These Indians lived in relative harmony in the valley they called "Ah-wah-nee" until the fateful Euro-American occupation of the Sierra foothills around 1850. Ahwahnee (as it is spelled now) probably means "place of a gaping mouth," although Lafayette Bunnell of the Mariposa Battalion reported that through hand signals the native people had indicated its meaning was "deep, grassy valley."

As friction between gold seekers and foothill Indians increased, anti-Indian sentiments blossomed. Groups from the Central Valley moved higher into the foothills, and conflict resulted between both Indians and whites and between rival Indian groups. As Tenaya and his fellows defiantly protected their mountain stronghold, violence did occur. The Mariposa Battalion was formed to locate, capture and relocate to reservations the native residents, and the story of its discovery of Yosemite Valley and its removal of the Indian people is well known.

The white soldiers called the Indians the "Yosemites," from the Miwok word "uzumati" or grizzly bear. (The natives called themselves the Ahwahneechees.) Some consider this a corruption of the Ahwahneechee word "Yo-che-ma-te" which means "some among them are killers." Whatever the true meaning, the local Indians were known as fierce fighters who lived in an area where grizzly bears were fairly common.

Following Tenaya's death in 1853, what was left of the band of Yosemite Indians dispersed to other locations. Some went east to the Mono Lake area, others joined neighboring peoples along the Tuolumne River. Never again did the remaining Yosemites gather together as a people.

Within twenty years, the number of native Indians living in the Yosemite area dwindled to below 50. With white settlement of Yosemite Valley and ever-increasing visitation, the native Miwok culture was irrevocably corrupted.

Hotelkeepers and other concessioners employed some of the Indians for odd jobs and manual labor, but the Yosemites were only tolerated at best.

A Gentle Lifestyle

During their hundreds of years of occupation of Yosemite Valley, the Yosemite Miwoks were remarkably gentle in their use of the land. There were at least 40 different camp spots on the floor of the Valley. Most of them were summer encampments only. Because of heavy snow and extremely cold temperatures, the bulk of the Valley residents moved to the El Portal area and the foothills below to pass the severe winter months.

The houses of the people were rude structures covered primarily by slabs of cedar bark. The typical house was a conical lean-to sporting three layers of bark and affording reasonable shelter from the elements. The Yosemite Miwoks also built earth-covered dance and sweat houses, and small elevated granaries for storing acorns and other edibles.

Native foodstuffs were hunted and gathered (no known cultivation was done). The staple of the Indian diet was acorn which was elaborately prepared and eaten as mush. Other vegetation such as mushrooms, ferns, clover and bulbs was also eaten. Fish and game included deer, squirrels, rabbits, rainbow trout and the Sacramento sucker. Some insects like certain fly larvae, caterpillars and grasshoppers were also considered delicacies.

Products of the Yosemite Indian culture included fairly coarse twined baskets and more fine coiled baskets with elaborate patterns, cradles, bows and arrows, obsidian tools and implements, bone awls and scrapers, and some ceremonial costumes. Today the only noticeable evidence of the habitation of Yosemite Valley by native peoples is the occasional discovery of an obsidian flake or a granite grinding hole.

Q: What is the shiny black substance used by the Indians for making arrowheads and other implements?
A: Obsidian, a volcanic glass common on the east side of the Sierra Nevada. The Yosemites would trade acorns and other items with their eastern neighbors for obsidian.

The Euro-American Occupation

Yosemite Valley was sighted by Euro-Americans for the first time in 1833. A party of explorers headed by Joseph Rutherford Walker was crossing the Sierra Nevada that fall, and in their efforts to determine the best route, several of the group came upon the north rim of the Valley. The cliffs were described as "more than a mile high," and after several efforts the mountaineers determined that they were "utterly impossible for a man to descend, to say nothing of our horses."

Some twenty years later, the Valley was finally entered by someone other than Native Americans.

In response to actions by the Yosemite Indians and their neighbors in defense of their homeland, a group of men was organized as the Mariposa Battalion to kill Indians as necessary and to transport survivors to reservations in the Central Valley. A punitive expedition was mounted in March of 1851, and their quest for Indians led the battalion into Yosemite Valley where they beheld what no other group of pioneers had seen before.

It wasn't long before the word began to spread about Yosemite's wonders. Letters from members of the Mariposa Battalion to San Francisco newspapers aroused the interest of James Mason Hutchings who organized the first tourist party to Yosemite Valley in 1855. He brought the artist, Thomas Ayres, who made sketches of the geologic features which Hutchings used to disseminate Yosemite's fame even more widely.

An increasing stream of visitors arrived primarily on foot and horseback, but as the years passed, wagon roads were developed to permit yet greater visitation. Hutchings became the chief entrepreneur and publicist for Yosemite, homesteading land and operating a hotel for early tourists. Other hotels and residences were built, livestock was grazed in the meadows, crops were planted, orchards were established, and Yosemite Valley was treated as no more than a resource to be exploited.

The State Grant

Fortunately, not everyone viewed the Valley as a capitalist's dream come true. Some amazingly farsighted persons took it upon themselves to work for the protection of Yosemite Valley for the public good. These early day conservationists, I.W. Raymond and Frederick Law Olmsted (the landscape architect who later designed New York's Central Park) prominent among them, appealed to Congress. Senator John Conness introduced a bill to grant Yosemite Valley and the Mariposa Grove of Big Trees to the State of California for preservation and protection. The bill was passed, and President Abraham Lincoln interrupted his preoccupation with the Civil War to sign the legislation on June 30, 1864.

It was a landmark event. Never before had a government set aside a piece of land for its inherent natural and scenic qualities to be preserved for the public use, resort and recreation "inalienable for all time." Yosemite became, in effect, the first state park and the first national park in the world. It unquestionably served as a model for the development of other parks and led to the birth of the National Park System as we know it today.

Public Management

Responsibility for management of the Yosemite Grant (as it came to be called) fell to a Board of Commissioners appointed by California's Governor and to the "Guardian" that the board hired. Yosemite's first Guardian was Galen Clark (see page 101). The 1860's and 70's saw improved access to the Valley thanks to the completion of several wagon roads, and the Guardian had to contend with an astounding rise in visitation.

Many new hostelries were built including the extravagant Cosmopolitan Saloon and Bathhouse, Black's Hotel, Leidig's Hotel, La Casa Nevada Hotel, the Stoneman House and others. Competition was fierce among the various operators, and unsuspecting visitors found themselves heavily lobbied by concessioners seeking their business.

Things in Yosemite were far from peaceful and quiet, however. Given the intense public interest in Yosemite as well as the disappointment of the original homesteaders who saw their opportunities to make a killing disappear, Yosemite politics were never boring. Several law suits were brought by individuals who were dispossessed by the Yosemite Grant (Hutchings foremost among them), and criticism was regularly levelled at the Board of Commissioners for their alleged poor management.

Greater Yosemite

While Yosemite Valley and the Big Trees had been recognized and protected, the thousands of acres of wilderness surrounding these relatively small park strongholds had not. Led by John Muir (see page 102) and by Easterner Robert Underwood Johnson (editor of the then influential *Century Magazine*), a group of preservationists began to focus attention on the need to protect the greater Yosemite area including the beautiful high country regions like Tuolumne Meadows.

As resource degradation such as mining, logging and stock grazing increased, so did the efforts of Yosemite champions. Muir and Johnson did their best to influence Congress and to inform the American people about the threats to Yosemite, and on October 1, 1890, the U.S. Government acknowledged the preciousness of these Sierra wildlands by enacting the law that established Yosemite National Park. Interestingly, Yosemite National Park did not include Yosemite Valley or the Mariposa Grove, but it encompassed an enormous area around them. The park was actually 25% larger than it is today.

The Army Takes Control

The brand new national park needed management, and in 1890, the National Park Service had not yet been established. It was determined that the U.S. Army would assume the administration of Yosemite (as they had at other National Parks), and members of the cavalry became a common sight in the park. Because much of the area was covered by a deep blanket of snow during the winter months, the Army limited its occupation of Yosemite to summers only. Usually soldiers from San Francisco would ride or march to and from their headquarters in Wawona each summer.

The duties of the cavalrymen were multiple and varied. They chased sheepherders from high country meadows, explored previously uncharted regions of the park blazing trails and preparing maps, surveyed boundaries, and prevented poachers from illegally taking park game. The work done by Army personnel was prodigious, and their mark on Yosemite's history was a major one.

During the Spanish-American War when many US troops were engaged, civilian rangers were hired by the Army to assist at the park. They were the first of their kind.

The existence of two different administrations, one for Yosemite Valley and the Big Trees, the other for the greater Yosemite National Park, inevitably led to duplication, overlap and conflict. Many individuals and organizations (including John Muir and the Sierra Club) began to push for a unification of all of Yosemite under the management of one entity.

A Single Yosemite

The mood of the public was apparently shared by lawmakers and government officials. In 1906 the federal government formally accepted the "recession" of Yosemite Valley and the Mariposa Grove of Big Trees from the State of California which act obviated the Yosemite Grant once and for all. The price of the agreement was the reduction in overall size of the park to conform it to natural boundaries and to exclude private mining and timber holdings. But at last there was one Yosemite National Park with a single administration.

The US Army continued its management of the park, moving its headquarters to Yosemite Valley (to a site near the present-day Yosemite Lodge). In 1914 a civilian administration was established, and the first "Park Rangers" were authorized and employed by the Department of the Interior.

The Army Years

The years between 1890 and 1914 were characterized by a transportation revolution. Regular stage lines began operation, and private wagons commonly made the trip to Yosemite. Visitation continued its remarkable expansion,

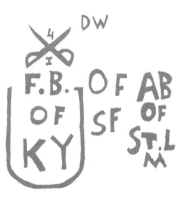

and the completion of the Yosemite Valley Railroad from Merced to El Portal in 1907 effectively heralded the end of the stagecoach era at Yosemite. But more earthshaking changes in transportation were still to come.

In 1900, the first automobile entered Yosemite Valley (albeit illegally). The US Army first officially allowed automobiles into the park in 1913, and when they came, they came with a vengeance. Two years later, all horse-drawn stages connecting train passengers to Yosemite Valley were replaced by motor stages. By 1920, two-thirds of all visitors were coming to Yosemite via private automobile.

The period also witnessed growth and proliferation of concessioner facilities. Public campgrounds were initiated, Camp Curry was established, Best's Studio was founded, and Camp Ahwahnee was built at the base of Sentinel Rock. Competition remained hot and heavy, and considerable conflict resulted between concessioners.

Finally, a regrettable chapter in Yosemite's history was written during the Army years. The famous and bitter battle over the damming of the Hetch Hetchy Valley was settled in 1913 with the enactment of the Raker Act. See page 55 for more about the Hetch Hetchy controversy.

Q: Who was the first permanent Euro-American resident of Yosemite Valley?
A: James Lamon who took up a preemption claim in the Valley's east end in 1859 and built a cabin. Apple trees he planted still grow near Curry Village and the stables.

The National Park Service

A major change came about in the National Park System with the creation of the National Park Service in 1916. It had been recognized that administration of the parks required more than the part-time attention of the Army and that there was a war to be fought in Europe. The National Park Service was the Interior Department's chosen alternative.

It was Frederick Law Olmsted, Jr., (whose father had been influential in the establishment of the 1864 Yosemite Grant) who proposed that the purpose of the new agency should be: "to conserve the scenery and the natural and historic objects and the wildlife therein, and to provide for the enjoyment of the same in such manner and by such means as will leave them unimpaired for the enjoyment of future generations." This phrase became the cornerstone of the act that created the NPS and guides the agency still.

The years following 1916 were significant not only for Yosemite but for all US National Parks because the basic policies of the agency were being developed and implemented. The process of interpreting the NPS mandate to preserve the parks while allowing for their use was ongoing. Yosemite consistently was the park where new ideas were first tested and applied.

Yosemite's new National Park Service Superintendent was Washington B. "Dusty" Lewis who was responsible for many innovations and changes at the park. During his twelve year tenure the concessions were consolidated under one principal operating company (The Yosemite Park & Curry Company), roads including the Tioga Road were improved and tolls eliminated, new accommodations were built in Yosemite Valley (Yosemite Lodge and the Ahwahnee Hotel) and at Glacier Point, a new administrative center was constructed, and modernization of utilities, roads and buildings was accomplished.

Interpretation

It was also shortly after the birth of the Park Service that Yosemite personnel inaugurated the educational program so familiar to park visitors today. Known as "interpretation," the original program was the inspiration of Dr. C.M. Goethe, and Harold Bryant and Loye Miller were hired as Yosemite's first "nature guides" in 1920. At the outset the interpretive program was pretty much limited to nature walks, but it has evolved to include visitor center displays, campfire programs, informal talks, multi-media presentations, and informational literature.

A logical extension of the interpretive program was the Yosemite Museum, plans for which were hatched about 1921. Several years later a permanent Museum was completed in the park thanks to a gift from the Laura Spelman Rockefeller Memorial. At the same time a Field School of Natural History was established in Yosemite to provide for the training of future interpreters and nature guides.

These formative years of the NPS reflected the realization that protection of the parks depended on a strong program of education designed to increase public awareness of the special values embodied by Yosemite and other outstanding natural areas. The Yosemite model has been emulated throughout the world and is still as vital as it was 60 years ago.

The Modern Years

The past fifty years in Yosemite have seen consistent management and burgeoning visitation. With scientific research and experience, resource policies have changed. Fire is no longer viewed as evil, wild animals are managed to be wild, and artificial attractions like the Fire Fall from Glacier Point have been eliminated.

The greatest challenge facing Yosemite today is its popularity. With over three million visitors each year, the park sometimes suffers from overcrowding, congestion and air pollution. Effects of these conditions are often resource degradation and a diminished experience for visitors. It can only be hoped that the coming years will provide solutions to these thorny problems and that Yosemite will long remain the preeminent national park in the world.

Further Reading

✳ *Discovery of the Yosemite* by Lafayette H. Bunnell. First published in 1911. Yosemite NP: Yosemite Association, 1990.

✳ *Yosemite: Its Discovery, Its Wonders and Its People* by Margaret Sanborn. Second edition. Yosemite NP: Yosemite Association, 1989.

✳ *The Yosemite* by John Muir. With photographs by Galen Rowell. First published in 1914. San Francisco: Sierra Club Books, 1989.

✳ *West of Eden: A History of Art and Literature in Yosemite* by David Robertson. Yosemite NP: Yosemite Association, 1984.

✳ *Yosemite Indians* by Elizabeth Godfrey. Revised edition. Yosemite NP: Yosemite Association, 1977.

Yosemite Firsts: A Centennial Chronology

✴ **1833** — Yosemite Valley was first seen by Euro-Americans. The Joseph Walker party in crossing the Sierra encountered a valley with "precipices more than a mile high" which were "impossible for a man to descend."

✴ **1851** — The Mariposa Battalion under the command of Major James Savage became the first group of pioneers to enter Yosemite Valley. They were pursuing "intransigent" Indians.

✴ **1852** — The Mariposa Grove of Giant Sequoias was first discovered by a party of prospectors.

✴ **1855** — The first tourist party visited Yosemite Valley with James Mason Hutchings as guide. Thomas Ayres, an artist with the group, made the first known sketches of Yosemite Valley.

✴ **1856** — The first permanent structure, The Lower Hotel, was built in Yosemite Valley at the base of Sentinel Rock. The first trail into Yosemite Valley was completed by Milton and Houston Mann.

✴ **1859** — The first photograph in Yosemite Valley was made by C. L. Weed. His subject was the Upper Hotel.

✴ **1864** — Yosemite Valley and the Mariposa Big Trees were set aside by the federal government as the first state park in the world. Florence Hutchings was the first white child to be born in Yosemite Valley.

✴ **1866** — Galen Clark was named the first Yosemite Guardian.

✴ **1868** — John Muir made his first trip to Yosemite.

✴ **1871** — The first ascent of Mt. Lyell, Yosemite's highest peak, was accomplished by J.B. Tileston on August 29.

✴ **1874** — The first road into Yosemite Valley, the Coulterville Road, was completed. The Big Oak Flat Road was finished a month later.

✴ **1875** — George Anderson made the first ascent of Half Dome before the installation of ropes or cables. The first public school was opened in Yosemite Valley.

✴ **1876** — John Muir's first article on the devastation of the Sierra Nevada by sheep was published.

✴ **1878** — The first public campgrounds were opened in Yosemite Valley by A. Harris near the site of the present-day Ahwahnee Hotel.

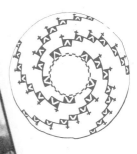

✳ **1890** — Yosemite National Park first established. The park did not include Yosemite Valley or the Mariposa Big Trees, but encompassed a large region around them.

✳ **1891** — The first telephones were installed in Yosemite Valley.

✳ **1892** — Trout were first planted in Yosemite waters by the California Fish and Game Commission.

✳ **1896** — Fire arms were first prohibited from the park.

✳ **1898** — The first civilian park ranger, Archie Leonard, was employed at Yosemite.

✳ **1900** — The first automobile (a Locomobile) was driven into Yosemite by Oliver Lippincott and Edward C. Russell.

✳ **1907** — The first railway line to Yosemite, the Yosemite Valley Railroad, began operation.

✳ **1913** — Automobiles were first "officially" admitted to Yosemite.

✳ **1915** — First appropriation for the construction of the John Muir Trail approved.

✳ **1916** — The National Park Service was first established. Washington B. Lewis was named the first N.P.S. Superintendent of Yosemite National Park.

✳ **1917** — The first High Sierra Camp, Tuolumne Meadows Lodge, was installed.

✳ **1919** — The first airplane, piloted by Lt. J.S. Krull, landed in Yosemite Valley on May 27.

✳ **1921** — The first installations in the Yosemite Museum were completed.

✳ **1926** — The Yosemite Museum first opened to the public.

✳ **1934** — The first water from the Hetch Hetchy Reservoir flowed into San Francisco.

✳ **1935** — Badger Pass Ski Area was first developed.

✳ **1940** — Ostrander Ski Hut was first opened for winter use.

✳ **1946** — The first ascent of the Lost Arrow Spire by four climbers was accomplished on September 2.

✳ **1949** — The first use of a helicopter for rescue purposes was made at Benson Lake to fly an injured boy to safety.

✳ **1951** — The first airplane planting of trout was done in Yosemite.

✳ **1954** — Park visitation exceeded the one million level for the first time in history; 1,008,031 visitors were recorded.

✳ **1958** — The first climb up the face of El Capitan was completed.

✳ **1961** — Pioneer Yosemite History Center first opened to the public.

✳ **1966** — New Yosemite Valley Visitor Center built.

✳ **1967** — For the first time over 2 million visitors were recorded at Yosemite.

✳ **1970** — The free shuttle bus system was initiated in Yosemite Valley.

✳ **1972** — The first asphalt was removed from the parking lot in front of the Yosemite Valley Visitor Center. The area was converted to use as a pedestrian mall.

✳ **1974** — Hang gliding was first officially allowed from Glacier Point. 170 flights were made.

✳ **1976** — The Tioga Road opened April 10, the first time it had been cleared at such an early date.

✳ **1980** — The Yosemite General Management Plan was completed and approved. It was the first systematically developed, long-range planning document for the park.

✳ **1981** — Captive-born Peregrine falcon chicks were first successfully reared in a nest on El Capitan.

✳ **1983** — The first-ever prescribed burn was accomplished in the Mariposa Grove of Big Trees.

✳ **1984** — Yosemite was named to the World Heritage List. The California Wilderness Bill designated 89% of the park as wilderness.

✳ **1986** — California bighorn sheep were first reintroduced into Yosemite.

✳ **1987** — Park visitation exceeded three million for the first time; 3,266,342 visitors were recorded.

✳ **1990** — Yosemite celebrated its first 100 years as a national park. Major forest fires raked the park during August.

Historical Sites in Yosemite Valley

The following locations have special historical significance or were the sites of early development in Yosemite Valley. They are listed in order of locale beginning at the west end of the Valley, continuing to the east along Southside Drive, focusing on the east end of Yosemite Valley, then heading back to the west along Northside Drive. In your explorations, remember that all cultural resources should be left unimpaired, and that digging and use of metal detectors are not allowed. Marker references are to small wooden posts that have been placed along Valley roads to indicate particular landmarks or attractions. See the map below for details.

✳ **Bridalveil Meadow (Marker V–13).** This spot is where the Mariposa Battalion camped in March of 1851. This party was in search of Indians and was the first group of whites ever to enter Yosemite Valley. Around a campfire here, the group proposed and applied the name "Yosemite" to this marvel of Nature's handiwork. It was also here that President Teddy Roosevelt and John Muir camped in 1903 and discussed the need to preserve our nation's wilderness areas.

✳ **Bridalveil Fall (Marker V–14** *which is just past the Highway 41 turnoff).* This is roughly the place where the wagon road from Wawona entered Yosemite Valley. Towards the Merced River through the trees, a large sewer plant operated for many years. The sewer plant was removed in 1987 and over three acres were freed of development. Yosemite Valley sewage is now carried by pipeline to a new processing facility in El Portal.

✳ **El Capitan View (Marker V–17:** *watch for a parking area on the left where trees grow out of the asphalt).* Just upriver from here is the site of the bear feeding platform used in the 1920's and 30's. Garbage was dumped on the lighted platform which drew feeding bears and gawking tourists each night. Enlightened managers have long since dispensed with the spectacle.

✳ **Sentinel Rock View (Marker V–18** *about 1.4 miles past El Capitan View on the right and left).* Here was a portion of Lower Yosemite Village which included the Yosemite Chapel (later moved to its present location east of here), Leidig's Hotel which operated from 1869 to 1888, and Camp Ahwahnee (1908–15). This is also the trailhead for James McCauley's Four Mile Trail to Glacier Point, where for several years a tollhouse was maintained to collect fees from hikers and horseback riders. Watch for the locust trees which are the only remnants of this earlier occupation.

✳ **Swinging Bridge Turnout** *(there is no marker here, but the turnout is about a quarter mile past V–18 on the left).* The remainder of Lower Yosemite Village was located here. Black's Hotel stood from 1869 through 1888, photographer George Fiske's residence and studio were near the river to the west, Galen Clark had a residence here, and the Coffman & Kenney Stables operated for several years. As well, a boardwalk nearly a half mile in length was constructed through the meadow to the east to connect the Upper and Lower Village areas.

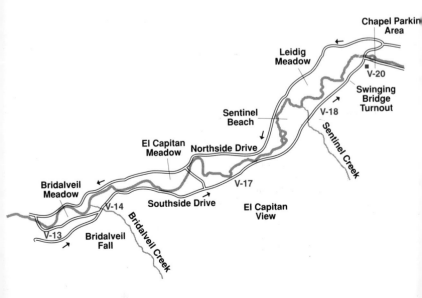

✳ **Chapel Parking Area (Marker V–20** *about one half mile beyond Swinging Bridge on the right).* This area was covered by extensive development from the 1860's until the 1950's. Here were the Upper Hotel (known at various times as Hutchings House, the Sentinel Hotel, and the Yosemite Falls Hotel), photographic studios (Boysen's, Foley's and Pillsbury's), Best's Studio, Degnan's Store and Restaurant, the world-famous Cosmopolitan Saloon, the Village Store and many other structures. In 1925, the "new" Yosemite Village site was selected (the present location) and an administration building, museum, post office and several artist studios were built. Slowly the Upper (old) Village was dismantled and razed. The Village Store was the last major building to go in 1959. The observant historian can still find plenty of evidence of Yosemite's yesteryears with a little exploring here.

✳ **Stoneman Meadow (Marker V–23** *near Curry Village).* This meadow has been the center of much activity over the years. Within it stood a large wooden hotel called the Stoneman House built by the State of California in 1886 that burned in 1896. James Lamon, a homesteader in the park's earliest days built a cabin near here, and planted two apple orchards in 1859. One now serves as the Curry Village parking lot, the other is behind the Curry Stables (shuttle bus stop #18). Stoneman Meadow will also be remembered as the site of a riot in 1970 which pitted young people against N.P.S. personnel in a clash over curfews, noise levels and lifestyles.

✳ **The Ahwahnee Hotel** *(Shuttle bus stop #4).* Before the present hotel was built, an active stable business was operated at this spot. Known as Kenneyville, the stable was extensive and there were horses, shops, barns and houses mingled here. When automo-

bile travel became popular, the need for such a large stable was eliminated. In 1926, to make way for the Ahwahnee, the stable was moved to its present location and the old buildings torn down. Many people are unaware that during World War II between 1943 and 1945 the Ahwahnee Hotel was closed to the public and converted to use as a Naval Convalescent Hospital. During that time almost 7,000 patients were rehabilitated.

✳ **Pioneer Cemetery** *(Just west and across the street from the Yosemite Museum in Yosemite Village).* This is the cemetery where, upon their deaths, local residents were buried between the 1870s and the 1950s. There's a wide variety of personalities interred here from Native Americans like Indian Lucy and Sally Ann Castagnetto to pioneer settlers and innkeepers like Galen Clark and James Mason Hutchings. A guide to the cemetery can be borrowed at the Visitor Center desk.

✳ **Yosemite Falls (Marker V–3).** In the forested area between the parking lot and Lower Yosemite Fall, James Mason Hutchings built a saw mill for preparation of lumber to upgrade his hotel. John Muir was employed to run the saw mill for a time, and constructed a cabin nearby to house himself. It featured running water; one strand of Yosemite Creek flowed right through it. Camp Yosemite, also known as Camp Lost Arrow, stood near the base of the fall and to its east from 1901 until 1915.

✳ **Yosemite Lodge (Marker V–4).** The lodge area was first developed as Army headquarters for the park in 1906. The facility included two large barracks buildings, two bath houses and lavatories, 156 tent frames and a parade ground. When the Army administration ended in 1914 so did the need for the headquarters, and they were converted to accommodate visitors in 1915.

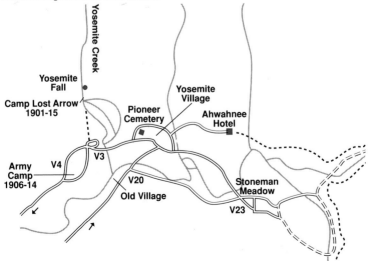

Yosemite's Centennial

*T*hroughout 1990 and until October, 1991, Yosemite will be celebrating its 100th anniversary as a national park. Most of present-day Yosemite was set aside as a public reserve by the federal government on October 1, 1890. Given the international significance of the park and the special place it holds in the hearts of people everywhere, the anniversary is truly cause for celebration. We should be thankful that Yosemite has been protected, that it exists in a fairly healthy condition despite ever-increasing visitation, and that people still recognize the need for its continued care.

Some would argue that the 1990 centennial is not as significant as is commonly believed. Yosemite's first centennial celebration was held in 1933 to commemorate the original sighting of Yosemite Valley from its rim by the Walker party 100 years before.

In 1964, a second centennial was feted, this on the 100th anniversary of the federal law that deeded to the State of California both Yosemite Valley and the Mariposa Grove of Giant Sequoias to be held as a state park. President Lincoln took a brief respite from the trials of the Civil War to sign the landmark legislation that made Yosemite the first natural area to be protected by a national government in recognition of its unique and valuable scenic resources. Given this history, many commentators have characterized Yosemite as the world's first national park and the model for state and national parks worldwide.

Even though Yosemite Valley and the Mariposa Grove had already been set aside, the passage of the 1890 Yosemite National Park legislation was a tremendously meaningful historical event, indeed. First, hundreds of thousands of acres surrounding the Valley and the Big Trees came under the protection of the US Government. Second, increasing impacts on Yosemite's high country such as sheep grazing, mining and other abuses were brought under control.

The strongest crusader for Yosemite National Park was John Muir (see page 102). Working with Robert Underwood Johnson, editor of *Century Magazine,* Muir campaigned hard with Eastern politicians for Yosemite's protection, railing against the sheep (which he called "hoofed locusts") and against increasing development. His efforts, which began in earnest in 1889, were rewarded quite quickly with the passage of the act and its signing on October 1, 1890.

There will probably be more Yosemite centennials. In 1905 and 1906, the boundaries of the federally administered park were trimmed and Yosemite Valley and the Mariposa Grove were assimilated to create a unified Yosemite National Park. This action ended the dual administration (state control of Yosemite Valley and the Mariposa Grove; federal control of the national park around them) that had existed since 1890. This date, then, marked the birth of the Yosemite National Park that we know today.

A number of special events will be held to pay tribute to Yosemite on its 100th birthday (at least this particular 100th birthday). Watch for workshops, lectures, art exhibits, symposia, programs and other activities with a centennial theme. Yosemite National Park staff will use the occasion to look to Yosemite's future and highlight the pivotal role the park has played in shaping the national park concept, park management policies in general and environmental awareness. Check the *Yosemite Guide* for dates and times for centennial events during your visit.

Q: Was Yosemite the nation's first national park?
A: Technically, no. Yellowstone National Park was established in 1872, the first time the "national park" designation was applied. But Yosemite had been set aside by the federal government eight years earlier to be protected for strictly nonutilitarian purposes.

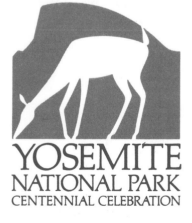

1890 – 1990

YOSEMITE
NATIONAL PARK
CENTENNIAL CELEBRATION

The Yosemite Hall of Fame

Chief Tenaya

When Yosemite Valley was first visited by Euro-Americans in 1851, they encountered the Yosemite Indians. Their leader was Chief Tenaya. He has been called not only a brave warrior but an unusual personality who maintained his authority over his people by his native influence and the the respect which he commanded.

Accounts have it that a tribal shaman warned Tenaya that "horsemen of the lowlands" (probably a reference to the Spaniards) represented the gravest threat to his people and should be guarded against. When in 1849 gold miners began entering the foothills and interacting with the native residents, Tenaya apparently felt threatened. He reportedly informed the invading whites that the Yosemites would be peaceable, but only if they could continue to occupy Yosemite Valley and not be disturbed.

Such an arrangement was obviously unacceptable to the new foothill residents. The Mariposa Battalion was dispatched to subdue the Yosemites, but met with only limited success. In May, 1851, the greatest portion of the band was rounded up and marched to a reservation in the Central Valley. Problems arose, the federal government never ratified a treaty, and by the end of the year, Tenaya and his people had either escaped or been permitted to return to Yosemite Valley.

The following year, a party of miners was allegedly attacked by the Indians in the Valley, and further efforts to remove them resulted. Tenaya's group fled to the high country of Yosemite and to the east side again. In 1853, they returned once more to Yosemite Valley, but their fate was practically sealed.

Despite his best efforts, Tenaya, the last chief of the Yosemites, was unable to protect his people and their homeland from the incursions of the whites. He was killed by stoning late in 1853. There are two versions of his death, but the must commonly accepted is that the Yosemites stole horses from their Eastern Sierran neighbors, who attacked in retribution. Tenaya's name is common in the park today and memorialized as a canyon, a lake and other features.

Galen Clark

Known as the "Guardian of Yosemite," Galen Clark was as intimately involved in Yosemite's early history as any other person. He moved to the park in 1856 at the age of 42 suffering from a debilitating lung disease which doctors had indicated would quickly end his life. The Yosemite fresh air and inspiring scenery must have been therapeutic; Clark lived to be 95.

He first homesteaded at Wawona developing his place as a stopping point on the stage route to Yosemite (Clark's Station). He first visited the Mariposa Grove of Giant Sequoias in 1857 with Milton Mann, then explored the trees and publicized them. He recognized the value and uniqueness of the Sequoias and Yosemite Valley, and worked to bring about the enactment of the Yosemite Grant, the 1864 law which set aside the Valley and Big Trees as the world's first state park.

In 1866, Galen Clark became the first "Yosemite Guardian," employed by the State of California to oversee the Grant. He continued in this job until the political winds changed in 1880 and a new Guardian was employed. He worked odd jobs for nine years and then was once again hired to be the Yosemite Guardian. His second term lasted seven years, and he closed out his life by guiding, writing books about the park, and helping wherever he could.

As Guardian, Clark made many needed improvements, worked to relocate homesteaders, and persevered in his efforts to protect Yosemite. John Muir called him "the best mountaineer I ever met . . . one of the most sincere tree-lovers I ever knew." Following his death, he was buried in the Yosemite Valley cemetary in a grave shaded by sequoias he planted himself and headed by a granite marker bearing his self-chiseled name.

James Mason Hutchings

James Hutchings will be remembered most for being Yosemite's first and best publicist. A native of England, he was attracted to Yosemite Valley very soon after its first entry by whites. In 1855, he organized and led the first "tourist" party to visit the Valley, bringing with him the artist Thomas Ayres who sketched the first non-Indian illustrations of Yosemite's wonders. Hutchings published the sketches and paired them with his descriptions of the place, drawing national attention to a previously unknown scenic treasure.

When his health failed, he, too, chose to come to Yosemite, and in 1862 purchased an existing hotel which became known as Hutchings House. The hotel was very primitive; only sheets of muslin hung to separate the rooms. Hutchings built a saw mill along Yosemite Creek to prepare the lumber for more effective partitions, and for a time employed John Muir to run the mill.

When the Yosemite Grant was set aside in 1864, Hutchings became embroiled in lengthy and bitter litigation with the government as a property owner dispossessed. His political fortunes changed, however, in 1880 when he was named to succeed Galen Clark as Yosemite Guardian. He worked in that capacity for four years.

Hutchings' many writings will live after him. His *Hutchings California Magazine* is full of historical gems, and he published a series of handbooks entitled *Guide to the Yosemite Valley and the Big Trees.* His most famous work is *In the Heart of the Sierras,* which is representative of the best travel writing of that era.

Killed in a wagon accident on the Old Big Oak Flat Road in Yosemite valley in 1902, Hutchings is buried in the Yosemite Valley cemetery.

John Muir

More than anyone else, John Muir has come to be recognized as the most significant individual in the history of Yosemite. This reputation is certainly deserved; Muir's contributions to the place through the years were considerable, particularly his efforts to create Yosemite National Park in 1890. He will also long be associated with the park thanks to his eloquent, loving writings.

John Muir first visited Yosemite in 1868 and returned the following summer to work as a shepherd in what would later become the park's high country. Late in 1869, he could no longer resist the lure of Yosemite Valley and found work doing odd jobs there for James Mason Hutchings. He built a small cabin on Yosemite Creek and began a long-term residence in his beloved Yosemite.

Muir roamed and studied the park, learning its aspects as intimately as he could. He became renowned as a guide, and entertained such visitors as Asa Gray, William Keith, Ralph Waldo Emerson, and other luminaries of the day. His marathon hikes with little or no provisions have become legendary. All along he recorded his experiences and documented the natural world around him.

In 1871, Muir published a newspaper article about Yosemite; it was the first of a series of articles and books he would write during his life. Topics of his writing included the glaciers, the forests, winter storms, and everything else about Yosemite that came to fascinate him. In the mid-70's, he moved from Yosemite, married and began a new life in Martinez.

In 1889, he returned to the park with Robert Underwood Johnson. It was during this visit that the two hatched a campaign to establish Yosemite National Park. Using articles, personal visits and other lobbying efforts, the two saw the 1890 act to create the national park through to its successful passage.

Muir was later to write *My First Summer in the Sierra* and *The Yosemite* (among many others), both of which would become Yosemite classics. His tireless work in opposition to the damming of the park's Hetch Hetchy Valley (a fight that he lost), drained him physically and contributed to his death in 1914.

David and Jennie Curry

The Curry name is synonymous with the concession operation in Yosemite, and this lively couple were pioneer innkeepers in the park. In 1899, they moved to California from Indiana and established a small camp in the eastern end of Yosemite Valley. Starting with seven tents for guests and a dining tent that seated 20, the Curry's initiated an enterprise that experienced immediate growth.

By the end of their first season, the camp size had increased to 25 tents and almost 300 guests had been accommodated. The operation soon became known as Camp Curry, and thanks to their warm hospitality and outgoing personalities, the Curry's prospered.

David Curry specialized in entertaining his guests with both disarming informality and brash showmanship. Every night at the campfire, people were encouraged to add wood to the fire, and while it burned, to tell stories or lead songs. Curry also revitalized the "Fire Fall," the spectacle which involved pushing burning embers from the brink of Glacier Point to create a stream of fire down the cliff face.

"Mother" Curry, as she was affectionately called, was considerably less flamboyant, but continued the Camp Curry tradition when David died in 1917. She was assisted by various family members and saw her camp grow to include lodging for 1,300 guests.

In 1925, the Curry Camping Company and the Yosemite National Park Company merged to form a single concession operation known as the Yosemite Park & Curry Co. Despite changes in ownership that name is still used today.

Ansel Adams

The man who has best communicated the beauty of Yosemite through photography during the 20th century is the late Ansel Adams. His images have been a source of inspiration, delight and enjoyment to millions of persons, and they have defined the Yosemite landscape for many. Further, he was a dogged conservationist who worked hard to protect the environment he photographed with such skill.

Interestingly, Ansel Adams was a gifted artist in two fields. He almost became a professional pianist, but the camera won out, particularly as Adams became more and more attached to Yosemite. He moved to the Valley in 1920 to run the Sierra Club Lodge and made the acquaintance of painter Harry Best, proprietor of Best's Studio, who allowed Ansel the use of a piano.

For several years, Adams worked as a "commercial" photographer doing publicity pictures for the Curry Co. and other such jobs. As the years passed, his promotional work gave way increasingly to his more "artistic" expression. His prints were offered for sale in gift shops and at Best's Studio, and before long he was gaining national recognition for his fine landscape work.

Many of his photographs were used to illustrate the beauty of natural areas that environmental groups hoped to have protected by Congress, and he undertook special assignments from the National Park Service to photograph the national parks. His landscapes became well-known for their detail, tonal ranges, unique composition and fine printing. A multitude of awards were bestowed upon Adams for his photographic excellence.

He remained active as a photographer and conservationist until his death in 1984, teaching, lecturing, lobbying and making new images all the while. Best's Studio is now operated as the Ansel Adams Gallery, and a peak on Yosemite's eastern boundary was named for him in 1985.

Selected Yosemite Place Names

Ahwahnee: The native Indians' name for both a large village near Yosemite Falls and for the greater Yosemite Valley. Those Indians were known as the Ahwahnechees. Lafayette Bunnell reported that the name meant *deep, grassy valley,* although this is unsubstantiated. Some linguists believe that "place of a gaping mouth" is a closer translation.

Big Oak Flat: A small town near Yosemite's northwestern boundary from which the Highway 120 route took its name. The massive oak (reportedly 10 feet in diameter) which inspired the name is long since dead, the victim of miners' axes in the 1860's.

Chilnualna: This name, common in the Wawona area, is of unknown origin and meaning. An unsupported theory suggests its meaning is *leaping water.*

Clark: Yosemite Valley's first guardian in 1864 and the discoverer of the Mariposa Grove of Big Trees was Galen Clark. His name now graces a mountain, a mountain range and other features in Yosemite.

Conness: A senator from California in the 1860's, John Conness introduced the bill in Congress that set aside Yosemite Valley and the Mariposa Big Trees as a state preserve. Mount Conness is an imposing peak on the park boundary north of Tioga Pass.

Crane Flat: Most probably named for a group of sand hill cranes encountered there by Lafayette Bunnell (John Muir also noted cranes at the location), although some assert the origin was a man named Crean who at one time resided at the spot.

Curry: David and Jennie "Mother" Curry established a small tent camp for the public in Yosemite Valley in 1899. It grew to become Camp Curry and later Curry Village. The merger of their operation with the Yosemite Park Company resulted in today's Yosemite Park & Curry Co.

Dana: J.D. Whitney's California Geological Survey named a prominent peak east of Tuolumne Meadows for James Dwight Dana in 1863. Dana was a Yale professor and considered the foremost American geologist of his time.

El Capitan: This massive granite cliff was named by the Mariposa Battalion in 1851. It is the Spanish equivalent of the native Indian name Too-tok-ah-noo-lah meaning *Rock Chief* or *Captain*. Other names assigned the rock at one time or another were Crane Mountain and Giant's Tower (Go Giants!).

El Portal: This is Spanish for *gateway* or *entrance,* and was used to name the terminus of the Yosemite Valley Railroad on the park's western doorstep. Now a small town on Highway 140, the site is slated to become the park's administrative headquarters.

Glen Aulin: James McCormick, at the behest of R.B. Marshall of the USGS, named this idyllic spot on the Tuolumne River with the Gaelic phrase for *beautiful valley or glen* in the early 1900's. A High Sierra Camp was built there in 1927.

Half Dome: Credit the Mariposa Battalion with describing this split mountain as a *half dome.* Of all the landmarks in Yosemite, Half Dome has worn the most names over the years, among them Rock of Ages, North Dome, South Dome, Sentinel Dome, Tis-sa-ack, Cleft Rock, Goddess of Liberty, Mt. Abraham Lincoln, and Spirit of the Valley. Somehow a t-shirt imprinted with the phrase "I climbed on top of the Goddess of Liberty" wouldn't quite work.

Happy Isles: One of Yosemite Valley's early Guardians named the three small islets on the Merced River for the emotions he enjoyed while exploring them ("no one can visit them without for the while forgetting the grinding strife of his world and being happy"). For years this was the site of a fish hatchery.

Hetch Hetchy: At one time a remarkably beautiful companion valley to Yosemite, Hetch Hetchy bears an Indian name which has been interpreted to have several meanings. The most popular is a kind of grass or plant with edible seeds which abounded in the valley, although some believe *Hetchy* means tree and *Hetch Hetchy* is descriptive of two yellow pine trees that grew at the entrance to the place. Hetch Hetchy was dammed by the damned City of San Francisco in the 1920's.

Illilouette: This French sounding name is actually an English translation (poor indeed!) of the Indian word *Too-lool-a-we-ack.* James Mason Hutchings opined that its meaning is "the place beyond which was the great rendezvous of the Yosemite Indians for hunting deer" (the great Miwok hunt club in the sky?).

Lembert: John Baptist Lembert was an early settler in the Tuolumne Meadows region. He built a cabin at the soda springs in Tuolumne, and his name is attached to the granite dome nearby.

Lyell: Yosemite's highest peak (13,114 feet) was named for Sir Charles Lyell, an eminent English geologist, by the California Geological Survey in 1863.

Mariposa: The Spanish word for *butterfly* which was first applied to a land grant, later the community, and then the county. Because they occurred in Mariposa County when Galen Clark discovered them in 1857, the sequoias at the south end of Yosemite were called the Mariposa Grove of Big Trees.

Merced: The Spanish name given the river originating in Yosemite's high country when it was crossed in the San Joaquin Valley by the Moraga party. Formally known as *El Rio de Nuestra Señora de la Merced* (River of Our Lady of Mercy), the title was applied five days after the feast day of Our Lady of Mercy in 1806. All other names utilizing *Merced* in Yosemite are derived from the river's name.

Mono: Derived from the Yokuts Indian word *monoi* or *monai* meaning *flies*. At what is now known as Mono Lake, the resident Indians harvested, ate and traded millions of the pupae of a fly — a favorite foodstuff of the native people of the region. The Shoshonean tribe grew to be known as the Mona or Mono Indians and many landmarks east of Yosemite bear this name.

Nevada: Assigned as a name to the waterfall on the Merced River by the Mariposa Battalion in 1851. The word signifies *snow* in Spanish, and members of the battalion felt that the name was appropriate because the fall was so close to the Sierra Nevada and because the white, foaming water was reminiscent of a vast avalanche of snow.

Olmsted: A turnout with a remarkable view from the Tioga Road near Tenaya Lake was named for both Frederick Law Olmsted and his son, Frederick Law Olmsted, Jr. The senior Olmsted was involved in the earliest development of the 1864 Yosemite Grant, and served as Chairman of the first Board of Yosemite Valley Commissioners. His son worked as an NPS planner in Yosemite and had a position on the Yosemite Advisory Board.

Sierra Nevada: This is the Spanish phrase for *snowy mountain range*. It was applied to California's greatest range of mountains by Father Pedro Font who glimpsed it from near Antioch in 1776. Because the word *Sierra* implies a series of mountains, it is both grammatically and politically incorrect to use the term "Sierras." If you do you will be castigated by self-righteous Yosemite word snobs.

Stoneman: A large hotel built by the State of California in 1885 once stood in the meadow just north of Curry Village. Known as the Stoneman House for then-Governor George Stoneman, it burned in 1896. The meadow and nearby bridge still bear the name.

Tenaya: The chief of the resident Indian tribe when the Mariposa Battalion entered Yosemite Valley in 1851 was named *Ten-ie-ya.* The battalion first encountered the native Americans living near the banks of a lake near Tuolumne Meadows which they called Tenaya Lake.

Tioga: This is an Iroquois Indian word meaning *where it forks, swift current* or *gate*. Apparently, miners at work on the Sierra crest near Yosemite established the Tioga Mining District in 1878, importing the name from Pennsylvania or New York.

Tuolumne: An Indian tribe residing in the Sierra foothills near Knights Ferry was known as "Taulamne," reportedly pronounced *Tu-ah-lum´-ne.* The Indian name was applied to the river originating in Yosemite which flowed through their territory.

Vogelsang: Col. Benson, an Army officer and acting Superintendent of Yosemite National Park from 1905 to 1908, named a peak south of Tuolumne Meadows for either Alexander Vogelsang or his brother Charles Vogelsang both of whom were affiliated with California Fish and Game. Vogelsang is German for *meadow in which birds sing,* an apt description of the site of the Vogelsang High Sierra Camp.

Wawona: The popular opinion is that the word is the Indian name for "big tree." The Indians viewed the trees as sacred and called them *Woh-woh´-nah.* The word is formed in imitation of the hooting of an owl which bird to the native people was the guardian spirit and deity of the sequoias.

White Wolf: A meadow on the old route of the Tioga Road was named by John Meyer who, while chasing Indians, came to the temporary camp of the band's chief. His name was *White Wolf.*

Yosemite: This name was assigned to the world's most beautiful valley by the Mariposa Battalion in 1851. They believed that the Yosemite people (as they were apparently known) who resided there, should have their tribe's name perpetuated in the designation of the valley. The exact meaning of the name is disputed, but Lafayette Bunnell, a member of the battalion, later wrote that the term signified "Grizzly Bear." He was informed that because grizzly bears frequented the territory occupied by the *Yosemites* and because the Indian band was skilled at killing the bears, the name was taken as an appropriate one for the tribe.

Further Reading

✻ *Yosemite Place Names* by Peter Browning. Lafayette, CA: Great West Books, 1988.

✻ *Place Names of the High Sierra* by Francis Farquhar. San Francisco: Sierra Club, 1926.

Getting to Yosemite

Most visitors to Yosemite arrive in private automobiles, but there are public transportation alternatives. Below are brief descriptions of those various alternatives. They are followed by detailed descriptions of the highway routes to Yosemite. If you need further information about transportation to Yosemite National Park call (209) 372-0265.

✶ **By Air** The major air terminal closest to Yosemite is Fresno's. A number of major airlines and several smaller ones serve Fresno, and a small airline also flies to Merced. Bus service is available from the Fresno Air Terminal and the Merced Airport on the Yosemite Gray Line daily. As well, rental cars are available at each location. For airline, bus or rental car reservations help call (209) 454-2080.

✶ **By Train** Train transportation is available to Yosemite from both Northern and Southern California. Originating in Oakland, an AMTRAK train carries passengers to Merced daily. Connection to Yosemite is made via the Yosemite Gray Line bus. For the return to Oakland, an AMTRAK train departs Merced every afternoon.

There are Southern California trains from both Los Angeles and San Diego on AMTRAK. The trip requires bus interconnects from Los Angeles to Bakersfield and from Fresno to Yosemite. Return travelers can catch a Yosemite Gray Line bus to Fresno for the AMTRAK trip to Bakersfield and connections to Las Vegas and Southern California. For train and bus reservations call (209) 454-2080 or 1-(800) USA-RAIL.

✶ **By Bus** At least two commercial bus carriers bring visitors to Yosemite on a daily basis. Yosemite Gray Line has routes from both Merced and Fresno on a daily basis. Call (800) 345-4950 (in California) or (209) 383-1563 for information or reservations. From Merced, travelers also may ride VIA Bus Lines to the park. Reservations should be made by calling (209) 722-0366. Greyhound connections to both Fresno or Merced can be easily made.

✶ **By Automobile** There are four major routes to Yosemite National Park. What follows are points of interest, restaurants and motels along each route. The list is not meant to be complete or exhaustive; rather, it reflects the preferences of the author. Because motels and restaurants are often short-lived, be sure to call ahead to avoid disappointment. Note: All directions and orientations assume that one is travelling toward Yosemite.

Highway 41 from Fresno

Oakhurst (45 miles north of Fresno):

Points of Interest

✶ **City Park and Chamber of Commerce:** Turn right just before the Chevron Station on your right as you enter town. Information is available from the Chamber, the city park will work for a picnic, and the local library's here, too.

✶ **Fresno Flats Historical Park:** Turn right at the only stop sign in the middle of town onto Road 426. Continue about half a mile to School Road (Road 427). Turn left and follow signs to this museum which includes a collection of old buildings depicting the lives of early settlers in the area. Hours are 1-3 pm, Wed. through Sun.

Restaurants

✶ **The Beach Club:** 40083 Highway 41 (on right at intersection with Highway 49), 683-5500. An odd location for a beach motif, but good food at reasonable prices.

✶ **Erna's Elderberry House:** Highway 41 & Victoria Lane (on left on final descent into Oakhurst), 683-6800. This is the proverbial diamond in the foothill rough. One of the few 5-star rated restaurants in California, featuring classic old European cuisine. Craig Claiborne of the N.Y. Times spent three days here and wrote rave reviews. But beware, you must dress up and dinners run about $45 per person.

✶ **The Junction Cafe:** 40276 Highway 41 (on left at the stop sign in the middle of town), 683-5558. Not much on decor, but good Italian food.

✶ **The Old Barn:** 41486 Old Barn Way (about a mile past town on the right, just off the highway), 683-2276. This is one of Oakhurst's institutions. Traditional dinners served in an old barn building with lots of antiques (you may be seated at a bed). Large portions and a relaxed atmosphere. Dinner entrees run $10-$15.

✶ **Ol' Kettle Restaurant:** 40650 Highway 41 (on left adjacent to the Shilo Inn, past the stop sign in the middle of town), 683-7505. Recently moved to this spot, the Kettle is renowned for its breakfast fare.

Motels

✻ **Oakhurst Lodge:** On left side of Highway 41 at the stop sign in the middle of town, 683-4417. 60 units; rates for two are $45 in winter, $50 in summer.

✻ **Shilo Inn:** 40644 Highway 41 (on left past the stop sign in the middle of town), 683-3555. 80 units, pool; rates for two are $63-$135 in winter, $69-$135 in summer.

✻ **Yosemite Gateway Best Western:** 40530 Highway 41 (on left past the stop sign in the middle of town), 683-2378. 92 units, pool, restaurant; rates for two are $60-95 year around.

Fish Camp (15 miles north of Oakhurst):

Points of Interest

✻ **Yosemite Mountain – Sugar Pine Railroad:** 56001 Highway 41 (one mile south of Fish Camp on the right), 683-7273. Take time out for a ride on an historic logging train. Utilizing Shay steam locomotives and Model A powered railcars, the railroad covers a four mile loop. Many special events are offered throughout the year. A fee is charged for the ride.

Restaurants

✻ **The Narrow Gauge Inn:** 48571 Highway 41 (on the right just past the Yosemite Mt. Railroad, one mile south of Fish Camp), 683-6446. A rustic but charming dining room with an excellent menu. Closed in winter.

Motels

✻ **Marriott's Tenaya Lodge:** 1122 Highway 41 (on the right as you enter Fish Camp), 683-6555. 242 rooms open in May, 1990, pool, restaurants; rates for two are $153-$165 in winter, $175-$190 in summer.

✻ **Narrow Gauge Inn:** 48571 Highway 41 (on the right just past the Yosemite Mt. Railroad, one mile south of Fish Camp), 683-7720. 27 rooms, pool; rates for two are $75-$105. The motel is closed in winter.

Highway 140 from Merced

Cathey's Valley (27 miles east of Merced):

Restaurants

✻ **Chibchas:** 2747 Highway 140 (on the left a short ways past the main gas station in Cathey's Valley), 966-2940. This is rich Columbian food followed with chocolatey coffee. Oddly authentic and good.

Mariposa (10 miles east of Cathey's Valley):

Points of Interest

✻ **California State Mining & Mineral Museum:** 5007 Fairgrounds Road (on the left side of Highway 49 at the Mariposa County Fairgrounds, about 1 mile south of town), 742-7625. A well-exhibited collection of minerals plus a mine tunnel and gold displays. An entrance fee is charged.

✻ **Mariposa County Courthouse:** Bullion Street (turn right on 8th Street near the middle of town, then left on Bullion), 966-4056. This handsome wooden building (erected in 1854) is the oldest courthouse in continuous use west of the Mississippi. Self-guided tours Monday through Friday.

✻ **Mariposa History Center:** 5116 Jesse Street (on the left side of Highway 140 towards the east end of town and next to the Bank of America), 966-2924. Historic displays and reconstructions of early-day Mariposa environments. Call for hours of operation.

Restaurants

✻ **The Bon Ton Cafe:** 7301 Highway 49 North (on the left in Bear Valley about seven miles north of town on Highway 49), 377-8229. A bit out of the way, but the experience of enjoying delicious Guatemalan food in an old Gold Rush-era building is worth it.

✻ **The China Station:** 5004 Highway 140 (on right side of the highway where it intersects with Highway 49 South), 966-3889. This doesn't rival big city restaurants, but it's adequate Chinese food.

✻ **Charles Street Dinner House:** On the left of Highway 140 at Seventh Street downtown, 966-2366. Good traditional food and plenty of it. A pretty sure bet.

Motels

✽ **Best Western Yosemite Way Station:** 4999 Highway 140 (on left where the highway intersects with Highway 49 South), 966-7545 or (800) 528-1234. 78 rooms, pool; rates for two are $60-$70.

✽ **Mariposa Lodge:** 5052 Highway 140 (on right about midway through town), 966-3607. 37 rooms, pool; rates for two are $45-$65.

✽ **Mother Lode Lodge:** 5051 Highway 140 (on left about midway through town), 966-2521. 12 rooms, pool, one kitchenette; rates for two are $48-$55.

El Portal (29 miles east of Mariposa):

Points of Interest

✽ **Site of Savage's Trading Post:** On the right side of Highway 140, 22 miles east of Mariposa, at the confluence of the South and Main Forks of the Merced River. This is the actual site of an early day trading post where the Indians and miners went for supplies and goods. There's a gift shop here now specializing in Indian arts and crafts. You'll also find the trailhead for a hike up the South Fork of the Merced that's ablaze with the colors of wildflowers in the spring. 379-2301.

✽ **Yosemite Travel Exhibit:** Turn left from Highway 140 onto El Portal Road and proceed one block to exhibit. Here are relics of early railroad activity in and around Yosemite, primarily old train cars and a locomotive. El Portal was the terminus of the Yosemite Valley Railroad.

Motels

✽ **Cedar Lodge:** On the right side of Highway 140, 25 miles east of Mariposa, 379-2612. 122 rooms, pool, restaurant, bar; rates for two are $70-$90.

✽ **Yosemite Redbud Lodge:** At Savage's Trading Post, on the right side of Highway 140, 22 miles east of Mariposa, 379- 2301. 8 rooms, some kitchenettes; rates for two are $55-$88.

✽ **Yosemite View Lodge:** On the right side of Higway 140 at the park boundary line, 379-2681 or (800) 321-5261. 91 rooms, pool, restaurant; rates for two are $45-$95.

Highway 120 from Manteca

Oakdale (20 miles east of Manteca):

Points of Interest

✽ **Hershey Chocolate Company:** 1400 S. Yosemite Avenue, 847-0381. Free half-hour tours of the chocolate factory are conducted Monday through Friday from 8 a.m. until 3 p.m. See kisses wrapped and huge vats of chocolate, and you may even get a treat when you're done.

Jamestown (32 miles east of Oakdale on Highway 108, about 6 miles east off the main route):

Points of Interest

✽ **Railtown 1897:** Fifth Avenue (just beyond town), 984-4641. This is a State Historic Park featuring a 26-acre roundhouse and shop complex with steam locomotives and rolling passenger cars that have served the Sierra Railroad and Mother Lode since 1897. Open from 10 a.m. to 5 p.m. during summer and on weekends in winter.

✽ **Downtown Jamestown:** Main Street Jamestown is lined with shops, restaurants and galleries housed in restored historic buildings. The Gold Rush theme predominates in this thriving tourist attraction.

Mileages to Yosemite Valley

Via Highway 41

From Los Angeles	313 miles
From Bakersfield	201 miles
From Fresno	94 miles
From Oakhurst	50 miles
From Fish Camp	37 miles

Via Highway 140

From Merced	81 miles
From Mariposa	43 miles
From El Portal	14 miles

THE COMPLETE GUIDEBOOK
TO YOSEMITE NATIONAL PARK

1992 Supplement

Please note the following changes or additions to this guidebook:

Page 8:

> TTY Room Reservations -
> 255-8345

> Weather and Road Information -
> 372-0200

> Recorded Camping Information -
> 372-0200

> MISTIX Camping Reservations -
> 1-800-365-2267

Page 12:

The campground reservation system is now administered by MISTIX. Forms to be used to make reservations by mail are available by writing: N.P.S. Information Office, Box 37127, Washington, D.C. 20013-7127; or MISTIX, Box 85705, San Diego, CA 92138-5705.

For telephone reservations, call 1-800-365-2267. Hours of operation are 7 a.m. to 4 p.m., Pacific time. You may charge to VISA, MasterCard, Discover Card or American Express.

Page 61:

The trailhead to Mono Pass is located 1.5 miles west of Tioga Pass at road marker T-37.

(over)

1992 Supplement
(continued)

Page 62:

The phone number for the High Sierra Desk at Yosemite Reservations is (209) 454-2002.

Page 67:

Tenaya Lake Walk-In Campground has been closed permanently.

Page 106:

Oakhurst Restaurant Changes:

The Beach Club restaurant in Oakhurst has closed.
The Junction Cafe in Oakhurst has closed.
The Old Barn restaurant in Oakhurst has closed.

Add: **Sierra City Grill:** Stage Coach Road & Highway 41 (just north of the 3-way stop in Oakhurst), 683-5636. This unpretentious establishment serves a delicious variety of grilled entrees at reasonable prices. Patio seating available.

Add: **Szechuan Restaurant:** 40484 Highway 41 (just south of the Best Western Motel). Very acceptable Chinese food that's right off the highway and right on the price. "Spicy" alternatives available throughout the menu.

Restaurants

❉ **Jamestown Hotel:** On Main Street, downtown, 984-3902. Serving "continental California cuisine" from 11:30 to 9 daily, with a Sunday brunch. Outdoor cafe in summer.

❉ **Hotel Willow Restaurant:** Main and Willow, downtown, 984-3998. Food for the "California gourmet" at dinner nightly. Sunday brunch. Good for families.

❉ **Cafe Smoke:** On Main Street, downtown, 984-3733. Good Mexican food and great Margaritas. Closed Mondays.

Moccasin (37 miles east of Oakdale on Highway 120):

Points of Interest

❉ **Moccasin Creek Fish Hatchery:** On the left side of Highway 49 about 100 feet south of its intersection with Highway 120, 989-2312. Take a self-guided tour of this facility (operated by the California Department of Fish and Game), which produces 1,000,000 catchable size rainbow trout annually for Sierra foothill reservoirs, streams and rivers. Open 7 am to 4 pm daily, year around.

Groveland (9 miles east of Moccasin):

Restaurants

❉ **Hotel Charlotte:** On the left side of Highway 120 in the center of downtown, 962-6455. They characterize their food as hearty California country cuisine.

❉ **Coffee Express:** On the left side of Highway 120 in the center of downtown, 962-7393. Serving breakfast and lunch only, but the homemade pies and sandwiches are delicious.

Buck Meadows (12 miles east of Groveland):

Restaurants

❉ **Buck Meadows Lodge:** 7647 Highway 120 (on the left where the road gets wide), 962-6366. Homestyle food served by some of the friendliest people in the mountains.

Motels

❉ **Buck Meadows Lodge:** 7647 Highway 120, 962-6366 or (800) 332-6300. 21 rooms, restaurant; rates for two are $55-$70.

Highway 120 from Lee Vining

Lee Vining (at intersection of Highways 120 and 395):

Points of Interest

❉ **Mono Lake County Park:** 5 miles north of Lee Vining on Highway 395. A great spot for a picnic with a trail down to the lakeshore.

❉ **Mono Lake Information Center:** Downtown Lee Vining, 647-6386. Offering free educational exhibits, slide shows and movies to visitors, plus a good bookstore.

Restaurants

❉ **Nicely's:** Downtown Lee Vining, (619) 647-6477. A family restaurant in the coffee shop style with no pretensions.

❉ **Tioga Pass Resort:** Nine miles west of Lee Vining on Highway 395, 372-4471. A local landmark, famous for its homemade pies (see page 68).

Motels

❉ **Best Western Lakeview Lodge:** On Highway 395 in downtown Lee Vining, (619) 647-6543 or (800) 528-1234. A nice motel run by even nicer people, the Banta's. 47 rooms, rates for 2 are $50-$70.

❉ **Tioga Pass Resort:** Nine miles west of Lee Vining on Highway 395, 372-4471. 10 housekeeping cabins and 4 motel-type units; rates for 2 are $310-460 per week.

Mileages to Yosemite Valley

Via Highway 120 from the West

From San Francisco	195 miles
From Sacramento	176 miles
From Stockton	127 miles
From Manteca	117 miles
From Oakdale	96 miles
From Groveland	49 miles

Via Highway 120 from the East

From Reno	218 miles
From Carson City	188 miles
From Bishop	146 miles
From Mammoth Lakes	106 miles
From Lee Vining	74 miles

Yosemite in Fiction

Since people started writing about it in the 1850s, Yosemite has figured as a grand locale for several works of fiction. From mass-appeal romances to beatnik epics to entangled mysteries, the array is an impressive one. The following is a list of some of the better and more unusual literary works with a Yosemite setting.

✻ **1. *The Forge of God*** by Greg Bear. New York: Tom Doherty Associates, 1987. This science fiction novel is set in 1997 when there are profound changes to the solar system and the earth is threatened with destruction. People migrate to Yosemite to await their imminent demise. The book climaxes with an enormous cataclysm brought on by seismic disruptions. There's a great description of the collapse of the Royal Arches, the blockage of Yosemite Falls, the burial of Curry Village and the destruction of Half Dome.

✻ **2. *Star Trek V: The Final Frontier*** by J.M. Dillard. Based on the screenplay by David Loughery. New York: Pocket Books, 1989. Media spin-off in reverse. A book that grew out of the movie, part of which was filmed in the park. In one episode, McCoy, Spock, and Kirk are on "shore leave" in Yosemite. Capt. Kirk attempts a free climb of El Capitan, apparently falls to his death, only to have Spock (wearing levitation boots) catch him by the ankles in mid-air.

✻ **3. *The Dharma Bums*** by Jack Kerouac. New York: The Viking Press, 1958. The beat generation goes hiking! Here's a classic account of a 1955 climb of Yosemite's Matterhorn Peak by Kerouac, Gary Snyder and John Montgomery, written as fiction. The description of two crazed beatniks bounding down the side of the Matterhorn, yodeling and laughing, is particularly joyful.

✻ **4. *The Affair of the Jade Monkey*** by Clifford Knight. New York: Dodd, Mead & Co., 1943. Detective Huntoon Rogers tracks a suspicious character to Yosemite National Park. A body is found in the backcountry, so Rogers joins a 7-day hiking party. One of the hikers is murdered and a small jade monkey appears in another's pack. Can Huntoon solve the case and thwart an enemy plot directed against the nation?

✻ **5. *Angels of Light*** by Jeffrey B. Long. New York: William Morrow & Co., 1987. Here's a Yosemite climbing novel with a twist. It's based loosely on the true story of the drug plane that crashed at Lower Merced Pass Lake in the park's backcountry. Before the rangers caught on, hundreds of pounds of marijuana were packed out by Yosemite climbers. The author characterizes it as the end of innocence for the park's climbing subculture.

✻ **6. *Images on Silver*** by Rayanne Moore. Toronto: Harlequin Books, 1984. Believe it or not, a Harlequin Romance set in Yosemite. Christy Reilly is a highly acclaimed wildlife photographer who meets Ranger Travis Jeffords. Travis keeps asking Christy why she has worked alone for so long. Christy's secret is something no man can understand.

✻ **7. *Four Boys in the Yosemite*** by Everett T. Tomlinson. Boston: Lothrop, Lee & Shepard Co, 1911. Billed as the story of the travels of four boys, this is didactic fiction. The author hoped to interest young readers in the doings of the boys and to inspire in those youngsters the desire to see America. To quote from the introduction: "Intelligent patriotism must be based upon knowledge, and 'seeing is believing.'"

✻ **8. *Nurse in Yosemite*** by Beatrice Warren. New York: Avalon Books, 1982. Nurse Doralee Dahlquist moves to Yosemite and takes a job at the medical clinic. All goes well until she falls for photographer Angus McGonigal. The conflict arises from fellow nurse Jan Stagnetto's claim that she will marry handsome Angus. Will Angus resist Jan's charms or will Doralee get dumped?

✻ **9. *A Body to Dye For*** by Grant Michaels. New York: St. Martin's Press, 1990. Believe it or not, this one's about a gay hairdresser/detective who finds the dead body of a Yosemite park ranger in the bed of one of his regular customers. In his efforts to solve the case, he follows leads back to Yosemite National Park, where his contacts in the gay world help him sort out a cast of colorful characters.

✻ **10. *Zanita: A Tale of the Yosemite*** by Therese Yelverton. New York: Hurd and Houghton, 1872. Yelverton, who called herself the Viscountess Avonmore, spent the summer of 1870 in Yosemite Valley. Among the acquaintances she made were John Muir and the James Mason Hutchings family. This novel is a romance of sorts with thinly disguised protagonists Kenmuir (Muir) and Zanita (Florence Hutchings).

Stay in Touch with Yosemite

Join the Association!

The Yosemite Association is a non-profit membership organization which supports a variety of educational, research and environmental projects at the park. Members receive a quarterly journal which keeps them informed about what to do and see in Yosemite National Park and about developments, issues and current events there. As well, a number of special, free member events are scheduled each year both inside and outside the park.

To generate revenues, the Association engages in a variety of programs. Through publication and sales of books and other materials (the Yosemite Association developed this guidebook), its educational mission is served and dollars are earned. Other activities include outdoor seminars, the Yosemite Theater program, the Art Activity Center and many others.

Each year the Yosemite Association provides substantial funding to the National Park Service with its earnings. In 1990, almost $300,000 has been committed to support many N.P.S. projects at Yosemite that would not otherwise be undertaken.

The membership component of the Association is a critical one to its success. Please consider joining thousands of other Yosemite lovers who are already enrolled by becoming a member. For more information call (209) 379-2317 or fill out and return the form provided below.

Member Benefits

As a member of the Yosemite Association, you will enjoy the following benefits:

✲ ***Yosemite,*** the Association journal published on a quarterly basis;

✲ **A 15% discount** on all books, maps, posters, calendars and publications stocked for sale by the Association;

✲ **A 10% discount** on most of the field seminars conducted by the Association in Yosemite National Park;

✲ **The opportunity to participate** in the annual Members' Meeting held in the park each fall, in the spring Open House, and in other Association activities;

✲ **An Association decal;**

✲ **A variety of other membership gifts** depending upon your membership level.

Membership dues are tax-deductible beyond the value of the benefits provided to the member.

YOSEMITE
ASSOCIATION

Please enroll me in the Yosemite Association as a . . .

- ☐ Regular Member $20.00
- ☐ Supporting Member $35.00
- ☐ Spouse add $5.00
- ☐ Contributing Member $50.00
- ☐ Sustaining Member $100.00
- ☐ Life Member $500.00
- ☐ Participating Life Member $1,000.00

Name *(please print)*: ______ Phone: ______

Address: ______ City: ______ State/Zip: ______

Enclosed is my check or money order for $ ______, or charge to my credit card

Bankamericard/VISA: Number ______ Expiration Date ______

MasterCard: Number ______ Expiration Date ______

Mail to:

Yosemite Association, Post Office Box 230, El Portal, CA 95318. 209/379-2646

For Office Use

Paid: Card # Exp. Date: Gift: File: Comp:

Index